You've Got This!

– Vital Career Skills That No One Will Teach You

Lisa McNulty

First published in the United Kingdom in 2025 by

The Choir Press

ISBN Paperback 978-1-78963-572-0

ISBN eBook 978-1-78963-573-7

Dedication

To Fiadh, who is wise beyond her years, and to Joseph, who is already familiar with getting letters from me.

You've got this.
Love, Mum x

Acknowledgements

I am indebted to those who read drafts of this book; you provided encouragement and invaluable feedback. Thanks to Alexandra Eastaugh, Caroline Hann, Ceri Evans, Colette Quinn, Eleanor Walsh, Eleni Skarpari, Emily Feibusch, Emily Lamont, Fred Gulliford, Geraint Williams, Harry Hicks, Holly Freeman, Jake Foster, Jasmine Smith, James Hicks, Joanne Haines, Matthew Taylor, Matt Townsend, Michael Graham, Natalie Berkhoff, Nimet Rener, Nina Stewart, Qas Meghjee, Sebastian Ma'ilei, Simon da Silva, Sophie Richardson, Tom and Jemma Aston.

The content for this book originated in the workshops I created some years ago for my junior colleagues in Deloitte. I'm grateful to them for their wholehearted participation and feedback, and to my fellow partners in the real estate team for their trust.

To the team at The Choir Press, especially Rachel Woodman and Ann-Marie Lowery, and to Jess Poole, who provided the illustrations. Thank you for your help in making this book a reality.

To Elaine Sammon. Without you spurring me on, I never would have finished this. Thank you for our Sunday chats.

Finally, to my family, the most important of all: thanks to my cousin Nancy for her faith in me, to my husband, David, for his unwavering belief, encouragement and support, and to Fiadh and Joseph for their patience when I start a sentence with 'Research shows ...' or 'Let me tell you a story ...' You two have brought me the greatest joy.

Alan Mulally on Career Success

In an interview with Alan R. Mulally, president and chief executive of Ford Motor,[1]

Q. What's your best career advice?

A. Don't manage your career. Follow your dream and contribute. Think about just exceeding expectations of every job you're being asked to do. Continually ask for feedback on how it's going. Ask everybody involved what you can do to do an even better job, and the world will beat down your door trying to ask you to do more and more.

I've never laid out a career. I never said I wanted to do this job and this job and this job, and frankly, I'd propose that you really don't know what a job is until you're in it. The most important thing is that you are open to really understanding what is expected, and also where you can make the biggest contribution. The more humble you become, and the more honored you are to serve, it allows you to really understand what you can do to make a bigger contribution.

---

1   https://www.nytimes.com/2009/09/06/business/06corner.html

Contents

Part 5: Where to Next?

Introduction

What is this book about?

This book contains the advice I wish someone had given me when I was building a career. By the time I left the global advisory firm where I'd spent almost 30 years, I'd become a Partner and Vice Chair, and I had led various businesses across the UK, Europe, Southeast Asia and the Middle East. Looking back, I could tell a story of smooth career progression, but that would be inaccurate and incomplete. Two truths stand out with the benefit of hindsight. One is that how I managed myself and handled my relationships with others was key to thriving at work. The other is that at several junctures, more self-reflection would have served me well.

Because being smart and working hard is not sufficient for success to follow. The evidence is clear: academic excellence is not a strong predictor of career success. Across industries, research shows that the correlation between grades and job performance is modest in the first year after college and trivial within a handful of years.[2] This isn't surprising. Academic grades rarely assess qualities like teamwork skills, or social and emotional intelligence, the skills that will build thriving careers.

When I shared what I had learnt about these skills through informal workshops with more junior colleagues, I found that these younger professionals valued these lessons:

---

2 https://www.nytimes.com/2018/12/08/opinion/college-gpa-career-success.html

'[these workshops are] very engaging – the use of personal examples … was very effective and the background was well researched, pitched at the right level and illuminating.'

'… my brain has been 'rewired' (in a good way) around the mindset I apply towards giving and receiving feedback … the sessions are very well thought through.'

But when my elder child, Joseph, was applying for internships, I wondered how he would learn these skills. It was unlikely he would sign up for any workshop designed by his mother. But perhaps he would read a letter or two if it addressed a work issue he was facing. And so, this book was born.

How to use this book

This book assumes you've landed a job where you want to thrive. If you are in your twenties and aren't sure that your career choices up until now have been right for you, I encourage you to read Meg Jay's *The Defining Decade: why your twenties matter and how to make the most of them now*. No matter how much money you might earn, on a cold, wet Tuesday morning in February, it's still going to be extra hard to get out of bed and go to work if you don't enjoy much of what you're doing.

If the mood takes you, feel free to read this book from cover to cover. However, it might be more useful if you first read this foreword and the table of contents so you can dip into the relevant letters when you have some specific issue you want to tackle. You'll see that the earlier letters are more relevant at the very start of your career, so you might want to skip ahead if you're already a few years in. And although the examples I give are based on my career working in a large advisory organisation, they address human issues we all struggle with at work, whether that's in a large organisation or a small one, in the private sector or in the public sector. As James Joyce said, 'In the particular is contained the universal.'

Whether you are forging your career, managing a team or interested in supporting your family members or friends in their careers, I hope this book provides helpful tips and food for thought. I'd like to hear from you. You can reach me through www.youvegotthis.today

Lisa McNulty
London
2025

PART 1
Getting Started

1.1 Preparing for your first day
– why getting along with your colleagues really matters

Dear Joseph,

So, you've landed a new job. Congratulations! You're feeling excited and a bit nervous because you'll be meeting some people for the first time, and undoubtedly you want to make a good impression. You want to show your new colleagues that the organisation made a good decision in hiring you – that you're smart and a hard worker. What you might be forgetting is that getting along with your colleagues is more than a 'nice to have'.

Competent Jerks And Lovable Fools

Researchers have shown that there are two criteria that impact how people choose a work partner: competence (do they know what they're doing?) and likeability (are they enjoyable to work with?).[3] These two criteria produce four archetypes: the lovable star whom everyone wants to work with, the incompetent jerk who is usually weeded out by the organisation, the competent jerk and the lovable fool.

Here's the interesting part. Although people *say* that they would choose the competent jerk to work with over the lovable fool, in practice that turns out not to be the case. If someone

---

3   *https://hbr.org/2005/06/competent-jerks-lovable-fools-and-the-formation-of-social-networks?autocomplete=true*

is strongly disliked, it doesn't matter how competent they are, people won't want to work with them. But if someone is likeable, their colleagues will seek out every little bit of competence they have to offer. This may sound illogical; we forgo the chance of accessing a jerk's competence because we don't want to deal with their unpleasant personality. But people enjoy working with those they like. Lovable fools strengthen team morale and encourage co-operation, while competent jerks erode trust and undermine the esprit de corps.

Why getting along with your colleagues really matters

Learning how to be a good team player, working effectively and communicating well with others are skills that are vital to your success. For a start, you are going to need to learn from those who have been doing the job for longer. If you aren't easy to work with, you reduce the chances of getting help to improve, being called onto interesting projects and being given greater responsibility so you can show what you can do. If your new colleagues don't want to spend time with you, you're going to struggle. You don't need to win a popularity contest or suck up to the boss, but you do need to be easy to work with if you're going to make the most of your abilities and education.

It took me a while to understand that, despite my good intentions, the impact I had on others was not always what I had hoped for. I needed to work on my so-called 'soft skills' if I wanted to progress into the senior ranks. Some of those lessons were painful, especially when I realised how my challenges up until then had been exacerbated by how I managed myself and handled my relationships with others. It became clear to me that these 'soft' skills should more rightly be called 'power skills' for the effect they can have. And they aren't easy to acquire because they demand self-awareness and a lot of practice.

Remember ... when you're preparing for your first day ...

1. A big part of your job will be learning, and you need other people to teach you.
2. Help others to want to help you by developing your power skills (read on!).

You've got this.
Love, Mum x

1.2 Your first day
– making a good first impression

Dear Joseph,

First impressions count and they're made very quickly, sometimes in a fraction of a second. You already know that when you have a first impression of someone, it endures and colours your subsequent perceptions.[4] You're going to be meeting new people, and while you're forming an impression of them, they'll be sizing you up.

In the early days of your new job, your goal is to enable your co-workers and manager to get a glimpse of the key aspects of the real you, those aspects that you want to convey as soon as possible. In broad terms, you'll want to show that you're pleasant to deal with (so smile occasionally!), you're punctual and listen well, and you ask questions to check your understanding. In general, avoid sharing your personal views on politics and religion.[5]

Here are a few other reminders of what you already know for those very early days.

In the office

When you're going into the office, dress appropriately. Ask what the dress code is beforehand if you aren't sure. Turn up on time or, even better, a few minutes early. Even if the dress

---

4   *https://howtoacademy.com/podcasts/malcolm-gladwell-how-to-make-a-good-first-impression/*

5   Though, of course, where religious observance will impact your working practices, you should communicate that as soon as you can.

code is casual, wear something that won't embarrass you if you're invited to join a meeting with people from outside the organisation.

If you're expected to shake hands, mirror the other person's handshake, whether it's firm or like a dead fish. (See more on this later in *Part 1, Building rapport.*) Look the other person in the eye when you're speaking with them. I don't mean you should stare but make eye contact from time to time.[6]

Listen carefully to what other people are saying and respond thoughtfully. Sometimes, we're so keen to make a good impression that we slip into transmit mode and forget to be receptive. And when you're speaking either on the phone or to a colleague, be conscious of your volume and how you might be affecting others.

Good manners are important. When you're going to get a coffee, ask the person next to you if they would like a drink. Don't push your way in front of others through the door or into the lift. I hope I've taught you to be respectful to everyone, whatever their position. I've heard of more than one occasion where an otherwise stellar applicant didn't get the job because they did not treat the receptionist or the administrative assistant with respect. All of these small steps oil the wheels of social interaction and make it easier to settle into a team.

Remote working

If your first day in your new job is remote working, check your internet service well in advance to make sure you won't have connection issues. Choose somewhere to work where you won't be disturbed, and ensure your backdrop won't be

---

6   I appreciate this advice may be inappropriate for neurodivergent readers and also in some cultural settings.

distracting for your online colleagues by pinning a suitable image or blurring your background. As with in-person work, get online on time and dress appropriately.

You might feel tempted to take every opportunity to work remotely. With no commute and easy access to the fridge, working from home is an attractive option. But I would recommend that, especially in the early years of your career, you take every opportunity to spend time with your colleagues in person. For the reasons I've set out before, you need to be able to build and sustain good relationships with your colleagues, and the best way to have a good relationship with someone is to spend time with them, in person. Not only will you be on hand to take up any opportunity that might arise, but you will also learn by observing more experienced colleagues at work.

What you might be forgetting

Different audiences

You'll likely join an existing team when you start your new job. That team will have a team culture that you need to understand if your social interactions are going to go smoothly. After all, your conversations with your friends and those with your dad and me aren't the same, because we are very different audiences. It's the same at work.

Unless you have worked in the team previously e.g., as a summer intern (in which case this advice would have applied then), it's advisable to be circumspect, especially in the early days. What is the informal team culture? Do they engage in vigorous debate about political issues of the day, or is their discussion limited to more banal topics?

Figure out how your team members work, e.g., are there coffee breaks when they chat but otherwise everyone is quiet while working at their desks? We are often so busy with our own internal dialogue and concerns that we invest only a small part of our attention in the here and now. But life has more depth and character when we pay attention, and your ability to get along with your colleagues will improve when you are interested in what is going on around you.

Of course, you should be yourself, and don't pretend to be something you're not. We humans have an innate ability to sniff out a fraud (although there have been enough financial scandals to know that we don't have a 100% success rate). But in the first few weeks of a new job, it is wise to remember that we have two ears and only one mouth; listen twice as much as you speak.

In the early days, your priority is to build relationships and interact with other team members. So try to resist the temptation to use a break as an opportunity to check your phone, even if others are on theirs, and don't use your headphones when you're at your desk until you have settled in.

Showing you're smart

It is natural to want to prove to your manager and colleagues that the organisation was right to hire you, and so you may be tempted to show how smart and knowledgeable you are. But before you do that, make a list of all the smart alecs you've met and loved. How much time do you want to spend with a know-it-all? Not long, I suspect.

I was less than a year into a new job in London when my boss (who would later become the firm's CEO) told me that I was 'irritating to work with'. Exhausted from working 18-hour days, I asked him what I needed to do to fix it. He said, 'You keep wanting to show how smart you are. I already know that you're smart, so the way you jump to answer every question is wearing. Can you just stop it?'

This useful (and painful) feedback made me aware of how I appeared to other people, and I was lucky my boss gave me that gift. My insecurity was irritating, and I realised that I may have appeared arrogant. I was horrified. From a purely social perspective, I wanted to fit in and be liked. But what my colleagues thought of me also mattered from a work viewpoint; if I came across as arrogant, they might avoid having me on their team altogether, reducing my chances of working on interesting projects.

When you want to contribute to a discussion, especially in the early days when you don't yet know your audience, ask yourself two questions before you speak: [7]

- Does what I'm about to say help the other person, or does it simply help me to look better/ smarter/ more interesting? If it's the latter, stop. No one needs to hear it. Brandishing your intellect is likely to alienate you from your colleagues.
- If what I'm about to say could help the other person, is now the right time to say it? From time to time, it's better to make your contribution later, perhaps when you're alone with your colleague or there are fewer people around. Only by getting to know how your manager and your team work together will you be able to choose the right moment. You may find that some managers are less receptive to input delivered later, so you're better to speak up straightaway.

With every new graduate intake in the advisory firm, it was apparent very quickly that some people were quieter than others. I learnt that these quieter team members were concerned that they were not saying enough. And this concern

---

7   This is similar to the Buddhist way of asking five questions before speaking; is what I am about to say true, helpful, kind (hoping for the best for everyone), gentle (so others can hear it) and timely? While you may consider that these are good questions to ask at any time, I think the two questions above are an acceptable shortcut.

was intensified when their more talkative colleagues appeared to be rewarded with more opportunities, at least in the first few months. But I observed that if there was any such advantage to talkative team members, it was short-lived.

Talking simply because there is an opportunity to do so is not a new habit for us humans. In *War and Peace*, written more than 150 years ago, Tolstoy describes the contribution of a General Armfeldt to a debate on military strategy: '... he was putting [the plan] forward now not really as a solution to the present problem, because it had lost all relevance, but merely because he had spotted an opportunity for speaking it.' Don't be a General Armfeldt.

At the end of the day, your colleagues will want to work with someone who is a team player, who is thoughtful about how they approach their work and who is reliable.[8] Some of the most impressive people I've worked with have been among the quietest of my colleagues. They took a moment before speaking to prepare what they wanted to say and how they wanted to say it. They didn't make a lot of noise but when they spoke, they were worth listening to. Within a few months they had established a reputation for being considered in their contributions and were actively sought out by teams looking for a new member. Whether you are naturally talkative or more reserved, contribute to be helpful rather than to make yourself look good, and remember that listening well is vital.

If you make a poor first impression

At some point in your career, you will screw up a first impression. Berating yourself for saying the wrong thing can ruin a night's sleep, but it won't give you a second chance with

---

8   Patrick Lencioni, in his book *The Ideal Team Player*, describes the ideal team player as someone who is emotionally intelligent (people smart), humble about their own capabilities and hungry for the success of the team.

a new person. In those circumstances, accept that you have work to do. If you've offended someone, apologise without trying to defend yourself. (See also *Part 4, Preparing to have a difficult conversation*.) After that, focus on doing your job to the best of your ability. Being reliable, polite and doing a good job was your plan anyway. It's just that now it's even more important while you make up for whatever mistake you've made. Over time, you'll build the reputation you want.

Remember ... in the early days of your new job ...

1. First impressions are made quickly and are hard to change. You will build your reputation from the day you join the team.
2. In these early days, don't distract your new colleagues with information that doesn't contribute to the reputation you want to build.
3. Listen at least twice as much as you speak. Making an occasional high-quality contribution is preferable to making noise.
4. If you've managed to screw up a first impression, apologise if you need to and then simply focus on doing your job as well as you can. It takes time to change a first impression, but it can be done.

You've got this.
Love, Mum x

1.3 Building rapport
– some tips to help you get other people talking

Dear Joseph,

To build relationships at work (and elsewhere), I can't overstate how effective it is to be interested in other people. Pay attention to their stories, however small, because from those you can build genuine relationships.

While it's key to get along with your peers (who are usually the people who are most similar to you), inevitably, you'll need to build a relationship with people who aren't your age and don't share your interests. This can be daunting, especially when the person is a good deal older and more experienced. You may be at a drinks reception, stuck in a lift or travelling in a taxi, so a conversation centred around work could feel odd, too serious or perhaps just a bit dull. But there are some easy steps you can take to develop a conversation the other person will enjoy.

The term 'rapport' describes a relationship between two people who have a good understanding of one another, and who can communicate well. Learning to build rapport with other people can help you form a bond quickly with virtually anyone you meet, and having this skill will benefit you in your career, as well as in other social arenas.

Don't forget, though, that building an initial rapport (as discussed here) is not the same as building a relationship. Building rapport is the first step, but you can't build a decent relationship in a single conversation with an 'express checkout' approach. A relationship takes time to build.

Making conversation with people who aren't like you

I remember feeling almost paralysed in these situations, racking my brain for something interesting to say. I tried various strategies. When I thought I might be 'stuck with' a senior client, I'd read the front page of the *Financial Times* so that at least I'd know the latest business news. I quickly realised that a person with that experience probably wasn't desperate for my (likely less-developed) views on the day's business news anyway. That said, to save yourself embarrassment, it's generally a good idea to listen to the news or read the headlines in the morning. That way, if there's been a newsworthy event of global or national significance overnight, you won't look like you live under a rock when someone mentions it.

A lot of people find it easy to strike up a conversation about sport. I know, Joseph, that you can talk about most sports, and it's a great topic *if* the other person is similarly interested. But not everyone is. I have never willingly participated in a sports discussion and even once brought a book to a Six Nations rugby match.

I also wanted to refrain from any kind of chat that could look sycophantic. I've always thought that sucking up carries a whiff of desperation about it. (As I became the more experienced person, I found it so uncomfortable when someone sucked up to me).

So, I tried politics, a subject that's super interesting to me but got me into a heated debate with the CFO of a significant American client. He was a committed Republican who brought up Ted Kennedy and the Chappaquiddick scandal. I was born after that incident and didn't know the ins and outs of it. Suffice it to say, I learnt the hard way: politics is not the way to go, not least because it can be so easy to misjudge another's political persuasion.

As the years passed and I had children of my own, I sometimes found a safe harbour by asking if the other person had children and developing the conversation from there. But I quickly discovered that if the answer to this question was negative, the atmosphere could become more strained. I decided that asking family-related questions wasn't worth the risk either.

Tips to make building rapport easier

Before we get into the specific tips, a word about introducing yourself: keep it short. People want to know your forename first, so make sure they can hear you. Perhaps explain your role briefly, e.g., 'I'm the junior on Ed's team,' but don't say too much after that. Give them a chance to speak. As your aim is to build rapport, you need to focus first on learning about the other person. You can talk more about yourself later.

1. Use the other person's name

Remembering someone's name has been shown to make people more likely to help you, more likely to buy from you, and it's seen as a compliment.[9] So, use someone's name in conversation (not all the time, obviously, as that would feel more like an interrogation). You're going to have to listen carefully when you're introduced. If you're nervous about how you come across so that you miss their name at first, or you instantly forget it, don't worry. As soon as you can, ask them again: 'I'm so sorry, I'm having a mind blank, and I forgot your name. Please remind me.' Then listen carefully and try to conjure up some way of remembering it. For example, 'Is that Ian spelt with one 'I' or the 'Iain' version?' It will help you remember the name later so you can use it in conversation, as well as showing the other person that you're actively engaging with them.

---

9   *What's in a Name? A Complimentary Means of Persuasion* from Journal of Consumer Research. *https://academic.oup.com/jcr/article-abstract/22/2/200/1822517*

2. *Listening well makes people feel that they are interesting*

We all know how awful it is to realise partway through what we believe to be an interesting anecdote that our companion is looking over our shoulder as if to find something/someone more interesting. There are few things more jarring and discomfiting.[10]

Active listening means taking part in the conversation and working on the rapport between you and your companion. When you were a child, we taught you that making conversation is like playing football. It's fun to have the ball, but it's only fun for others if you remember to pass it back.

In conversation, it's a good idea to add something to the ball of conversation before you hand it back. Listen and play back some of what you've heard. For example, 'So, you're training for a marathon?' You might admit you're in awe of anyone running that distance and ask 'What made you decide to do that? Have you always been a runner?' This type of conversation can lead anywhere. For example, your companion may confess they find it easier with family and work commitments to run than to play a team sport as they did at college. 'Which sport did you play?' you might ask next.

3. *Mirroring and matching*

When we notice another person's emotions and then try to match their mood (positive or negative) and their energy (high or low), we exhibit emotional intelligence. I don't mean

---

10 When I was younger and noticed this, I tried to make my story more interesting, investing more energy in the telling of it. Now that I'm older and believe myself to be wiser, when I perceive that someone isn't listening, I stop speaking. That allows them to excuse themselves if they want to leave or to ask me to continue if they want to listen. It might feel very uncomfortable to have that break, but remember that a second or two is not actually a long time at all. See also *Part 2, Listening*.

that if your companion is cranky, you would immediately become grumpy; that would likely exacerbate their mood. But with emotional intelligence, you would notice their mood and acknowledge it by dialling down your ebullience and perhaps asking if there's something you can help with.

Have you ever noticed that when good friends are together, they tend to act and even sound alike? There's a simple evolutionary mechanism behind this phenomenon. Research shows that mirroring[11] and matching, that is, copying other people's body language, mannerisms, and repeating their words, helps to build trust and establishes rapport, making you seem more likeable to them. In fact, in a sales situation, a prospective client is more likely to buy from you if you mimic their speech and behaviour patterns, and they will feel more positive about you afterwards![12] The reason for this is that people feel most comfortable around others who are like them. And the more someone believes you're like them, the easier it is to develop trust and rapport on a subconscious level.

Mirroring and matching differ in the degree or level of emulation, with matching being a less specific imitation of the other person and not an exact reflection. I recommend you focus on matching because it's easier to do and less likely to be noticeable to your companion. The easiest behaviours to imitate are those relating to posture (including proximity) and vocal patterns.

---

11 The mirroring technique means that you become an exact mirror of your conversation partner. If he crosses his arms with the right arm over the left arm, you mirror this position when you cross your left arm over the right arm. It's like the person is looking in a mirror: your physiology is a complete reflection of theirs. When you're mirroring the words of another person, you respond with the same words that they have used.

12 https://www.researchgate.net/publication/232934334_The_Convergence_of_Mirroring_andEmpathy_Communications_Training_in_Business-to-Business_Personal_Selling_Persuasion_Efforts

So, if a person leans in towards you while they speak, you lean in too. If they sit up straight, you don't slouch. If they give you the dead-fish handshake, you do the same. You speak at roughly the same speed and use similar gestures as your companion. If they use more informal language, you should do the same.

But be careful. Don't always match their gesture or speech pattern exactly, and when you do match, don't do it immediately, or it will look like you are playing the monkey game. You can delay an action by a few seconds. For example, if the person shifts their position to lean back, you can match it a little later.

Reflecting on my career, I believe I did use these techniques when meeting new people, albeit subconsciously. However, I remember the first time I used them deliberately. At the time, I had to negotiate a budget with a man I loathed, and I suspected the feeling was mutual. I concluded that there was nothing to be lost in trying the matching technique in our discussion. I don't know if he was in an unusually good mood or if the matching worked, but we reached an agreement more quickly than I could have hoped for.

4. *Get them to talk about themselves*

As a general conversation starter, I must admit that I often used to ask new people, 'What do you do?' Now I realise that that can be a terrible question. If they're having a bad patch at work, they won't want to talk about it, so the question elicits a monosyllabic answer – or, even worse, an emotional rant, and you don't know how to respond. In the social arena, this question isn't helpful to those people who are in between jobs or whose time is taken up with caring responsibilities.

A good question in almost any situation where you have to make conversation is 'Tell me, what's been keeping you busy lately?' You can add 'outside of work' if you're talking to a fellow professiosnal. This question has two benefits. First, it allows the responder to choose something *they* want to talk about. A CEO may be excited about planning a holiday. You might have been to that destination yourself or, if not, you can ask why they chose to travel there. Either way, the conversation is easy. The other benefit is that it gets the other person talking, so you will be learning information about them that will help you build a relationship. They'll enjoy themselves too because, whether we like to admit it or not, we love to talk about ourselves.[13]

Depending on the circumstances and how much you know about your companion, you can also ask how they decided to enter the field they're in now, or you can use something as banal as the weather to lead you into an open question, e.g., 'I'm sick of the rain; a holiday would be nice. What was your best holiday?' 'What do you like to do when you're not working?' The good thing about these open questions is that your companion has complete freedom to choose their answer.

But don't ask a question as a pretext to indulge yourself in your favourite topic. I used to work with someone who would often ask me about my children, but only as a pretext for him to talk at length about his children. This is called conversational narcissism.[14] Once I realised he always did this, I did my best to steer clear of him.

5. *Ask for advice*

Depending on the experience of the other person, you could ask for professional advice (e.g., 'I'm thinking of doing an

---

13 https://www.scientificamerican.com/article/the-neuroscience-of-everybody-favorite-topic-themselves/

14 *https://www.researchgate.net/publication/248924932_Conversational_narcissism*

MBA. Have you done one? Would you recommend it?'). Or you could ask for personal advice. 'My girlfriend wants us to go on a walking holiday, but I'm concerned that it'll be tiring, and we both need a rest. Have you ever been on a vacation like that? What did you think?' Such requests give the impression that you value that person's opinion, and it also gives them something to talk about.[15]

6. *Ask someone to do you a favour*

One of the first people to write about how this can help build rapport was Benjamin Franklin, a significant figure in US history. He described in his autobiography how he dealt with the animosity of a rival legislator. After hearing that his rival had a rare book in his library, Franklin wrote to his rival and asked whether he could borrow the book for a few days. The rival agreed, and a week later Franklin returned the book, with a letter expressing how much he liked it. The next time the two met, Franklin's rival spoke to him with 'great civility' and showed a willingness to help him in other matters, leading to the two men becoming good friends. Franklin consequently stated that 'He that has once done you a kindness will be more ready to do you another, than he whom you yourself have obliged.'

This is known as the Benjamin Franklin effect, a cognitive bias that causes people to like someone *more* after they've done that person a favour, especially if they previously disliked that person or felt neutral towards them. We experience this effect primarily because when we do someone a favour, to avoid a state of cognitive dissonance, our mind tries to justify this behaviour by deciding that we must like that person.

---

15 Hopefully, it goes without saying that the advice sought shouldn't be too personal!

Research shows that we tend to underestimate people's willingness to agree to help, so don't feel bad about asking for something.[16] Also, in general, the scope of the favour often doesn't matter as much as the favour itself. It's best to ask for a small favour, like a recommendation for a restaurant or book. Obviously, most people appreciate it if we do a favour for them, no matter how small. So don't be afraid to offer that if it feels right to do so.

7. *Keep anecdotes short*

Not much to say here. Don't tell a long story, even if the punchline is hilarious. You need to know someone well to be sure of their attention span and sense of humour. And if you do tell a story, choose one that can resonate with your companion and leave space for them to share their perspective. That way, you can start to establish a connection by finding common ground.

What if the conversation doesn't flow?

In Charles Duhigg's book *Supercommunicators, How to Unlock the Secret Language of Connection*, he explains that if your companion leans towards you, makes eye contact, smiles or interrupts, these are all signals that they want to accept your invitation to a conversation. We often don't appreciate an interruption, but it usually means your companion wants to add something to the conversation, which is a positive response. If, on the other hand, your companion has a passive expression, isn't looking at you and takes in your comments without adding thoughts of their own, this indicates that they don't want to engage in this conversation with you.

---

16   *https://news.stanford.edu/stories/2022/09/asking-help-hard-people-want-help-realize*

A lack of engagement doesn't mean that your companion has taken a dislike to you, so try not to take this personally. It may be that you need to move the conversation on to another topic, or it might simply be that your companion has a lot on their mind and now is not the time for any conversation.

On leaving … and the next time

It helps to build rapport if, on leaving a conversation, you can refer to something that seemed important to your companion, such as 'I hope all goes well for your son tomorrow in his senior school interview' or 'Have a great time in Cape Town.' It shows you listened, and it's even better if, when you meet them the next time, you remember to ask how the interview or holiday went. I used to keep notes of all my client conversations so that I was able to remember things like this when I met them next. Making this small effort to be thoughtful helped build a relationship.

Remember … when you're building rapport …

1. Listen well, use the other person's name from time to time and ask follow-up questions.
2. Be mindful of the other's physical posture and speech patterns and try to match these.
3. Don't worry about making yourself interesting. Instead, have your companions talk about themselves and focus your attention on being interested in their responses. They'll enjoy it and you'll learn something.
4. Asking for advice or a (small) favour can help build a relationship.

You've got this.
Love, Mum x

1.4 Earning trust

Dear Joseph,

We've talked about teamwork and why getting along with others is so important. Apart from the social benefits of fitting in, you will need more senior colleagues to help you learn and progress. And often you will learn most when your colleagues delegate to you. To do that, they will need to trust you. And there's no shortcut: trust must be earned, and you're going to have to work at it.

What does trust mean?

Unlike other animals, humans have two neurological idiosyncrasies that allow us to trust and collaborate with people outside our immediate social group. First, parts of the cortex in our brains let us transport ourselves into someone else's mind: 'If I were her, I would do *this*.' Psychologists call this the theory of mind. It lets us forecast others' actions so that we can coordinate our behaviour with theirs. The second idiosyncrasy is empathy, our ability to share other people's emotions. We're wired to absorb social information and understand others' motivations (though we can still get it wrong; see later in this part, *How it's easy to be misunderstood*).

To trust someone unfamiliar, our brains build a model of what the person is likely to do and why. In other words, we use both theory of mind and empathy during every collaboration. And the other person intuitively does this about us, too. That means humans are constantly engaged in a two-sided trust game: 'Should I trust you?' and 'How much do you trust me?'[17] The more we get to know someone and the more we work together, the more confident we can be in the mental model we've built to predict their actions. Some colleagues may come to trust you more quickly than others. Perhaps you've shown yourself to be reliable on a couple of occasions, and that's enough for them to trust you on more complicated projects. Others might need longer. But make no mistake. Trust is a fragile and dynamic thing that requires ongoing effort and attention.

Four aspects to trust

So how do you earn someone's trust? The answer is simple but not easy. You'll need to make a consistent effort to practise the following four behaviours.

The first is care. When someone trusts you, they believe that you care about them, and that you know and respect what is important to them. If you are too focused on yourself and your priorities, they won't believe that you care about them. Show people that their opinions matter to you, and prioritise the team so that you share any credit, but own up to your mistakes.

The second is reliability: when you're trusted, people know that they can count on you to deliver what you promise. To do this, you must understand what is entailed in their request so that you don't overpromise. Ask questions to confirm your understanding, and check that the two of you have the same expectations of a situation. Mistrust can start to creep in if there are different expectations.

Sincerity is an important element of trust: you should mean what you say and say what you mean.

---

17   https://hbr.org/2019/07/how-our-brains-decide-when-to-trust

The fourth aspect is competence. Only commit to doing something you're competent to do, and admit readily when you need help to learn to do anything else.

It's impossible to overstate the importance of good communication underpinning each of these aspects.

Owning up to a mistake

Good communication is necessary but not sufficient. If you want to be trusted, you have to be accountable. That means that you must be willing to take responsibility promptly, apologise and make amends when you make a mistake. And yes, that's a when, not an if: you are only human and you *will* make mistakes. The only time my colleagues and I struggled to promote a competent colleague was when we weren't convinced that they would own up promptly when they'd made a mistake and we thought that instead they would try to cover up the error and attempt to fix it themselves. For these purposes, we didn't mean an error that could be fixed in a few minutes. We meant a mistake with potentially significant consequences where we, the more senior colleagues, would want to marshal our resources to address any problem. And we could only do that if we knew about it.

Owning up to a potentially significant mistake was something I've had to do myself. Here's one example. Shortly after my return from my maternity leave with your sister, I discovered that I had made a mistake a few years earlier, a few weeks after I'd returned from my maternity leave with you. In response to two client queries, I had focused on the technically more difficult question and had not taken the time to fully appreciate the implications of the easier question to which I had given a brief and incorrect answer. This mistake had a potentially enormous financial implication for my client. As soon as I saw my earlier advice, my heart sank.

I felt sick, terrified and unable to think clearly. Here's what happened next.

First, I conferred with the team who worked with me on this client. We talked through the issue and agreed that I had given incorrect advice. There was no easy fix, and if the client had proceeded as they had suggested in their email, the implications could be disastrous. I called my boss to tell him. His reassurance that no one is infallible was cold comfort. But he was supportive and helped me involve some senior colleagues whose advice and technical nous I needed. For a few weeks, it wasn't clear that we could fix it. I could barely sleep or eat, losing five kilos in ten days. But with the help of my capable colleagues, all was eventually resolved. I was never castigated for my mistake and, indeed, in my appraisal later that year, the only reference to the event was to praise me for having drawn attention to my error so promptly. Instead of struggling to fix something from a place of stress and worry (and when my judgement would not have been at its best), my honesty enabled the error to be rectified. In my experience, most mistakes are fixable, and even for those that aren't, the consequences can be better managed when more senior colleagues are made aware of them earlier.

All of this is to say that when you realise you've made a mistake, own up straightaway to your colleagues. In doing so, you will build trust. Don't try to hide it and fix it yourself. The chances are very high that your mistake will come to light, and then, the cover-up can be perceived as worse than the crime.

If your team is one where your manager punishes you for making a mistake and there is a culture of blame rather than one of support and learning, you probably need to consider if this team is the right place for you. (See *Part 5, Is this the right job for me?* and *Taking care of yourself is primarily your job*.)

Weak managers tend to blame others when things go wrong, and working for someone like that is unlikely to end well.

Remember ... when you're trying to earn the trust of your new colleagues ...

1. There is no shortcut, and maintaining trust, once earned, takes ongoing effort.
2. Care about your colleagues, be reliable, be sincere and don't overpromise.
3. Above all, be proactive in your communication, especially if you've made a mistake. No one is infallible, so mistakes can be forgiven. But delays and cover-ups destroy trust.

You've got this.
Love, Mum x

1.5 Taking instruction and prioritising tasks
– why asking questions is a good habit

Dear Joseph,

After the initial on-boarding and training, you'll be given some tasks to do. Unless your job is writing academic papers like you did in college, or your new job is the same as your last, you will almost certainly not know enough straightaway to do the job you've been hired for.

Where appropriate it's a good idea to write down what you're being asked to do, unless it is something simple and unforgettable. Taking notes gives you something to refer to without asking your manager to repeat herself. It also shows that you are taking your work seriously.

In the beginning, it might feel like you're being given 'busywork', that is work which appears to be of little or no value but which gives you something to do; the tasks may be dull, administrative and don't need someone educated or trained to your level to complete them. However, by taking a narrow view of this type of task, you risk missing something important. If you can't take instructions for a simple task, who is going to trust you with something more complex? Remember, you will start creating your reputation immediately. Once made, a reputation tends to endure unless and until there's overwhelming evidence to contradict it, and even then, it may linger for longer than might be fair.

So, however dull or administrative the task, try to do a good job. Many years ago, I worked with a talented graduate who had a first-class degree in law from a prestigious university. In his first month or so, like the rest of us, he was allocated a fair amount of photocopying (yes, that was a thing back in the nineties). Deciding that these tasks were meaningless and irrelevant, he took no care, including not noticing that sometimes the material was double-sided. He stayed for three years until he earned his professional qualifications and left shortly thereafter without any meaningful experience. No manager was prepared to trust him with challenging work when he had shown he couldn't complete a simple task properly. His intellect and academic record were wasted. Because the top priority of his senior colleagues was to serve their clients, teaching him useful skills was not so important when he had shown so little interest in doing a good job.

Also, when you aren't busy, don't be afraid to ask how you can help, even if it's just an admin task. Pitching in when everyone is busy is a behaviour universally appreciated so don't be shy.

Showing I'm able to do the job

It seems to me that a lot of the key skills needed to progress in most careers need to be learnt through experience. Provided you have listened carefully, there is no shame in asking questions. Indeed, asking questions shows a willingness to learn that is professionally attractive to your work colleagues.

Understanding the context

Let's say your manager asks you to do some research on Margaret Thatcher's election victory in 1979. That sounds straightforward and interesting to a history and politics graduate, and you are itching to get started. But stop and ask yourself some questions.

What does your manager want this research for? Understanding the context is key to doing a good job. How is your work going to be used? Do you think it's a technical research note that is intended to test your knowledge of politics and history? This is unlikely; you already have a degree in those subjects, so why would she waste her time and yours on a test?

Perhaps your manager is going to use your research to inform an in-house training session, so will she want lots of detail? Or perhaps she will use it for a relatively uninformed client? Will she be preparing a presentation or a one-page summary for clients, or an in-depth addendum to another paper?

In the early days of your career, with little experience, you may find it hard to 'add value' (as some books will advise). But you can always be thoughtful about your manager's request. Zoom out and consider the audience and the objective of the work. Would statistics be more readily understood in a graph than in a table? If she's going to give a presentation, does she want slides to speak to, or a document to circulate to the audience afterwards? Depending on the purpose, your work may be more helpful in a properly referenced bullet point summary than in a densely worded document. You might ask, 'So that I can give you something helpful, can you please let me know a bit more about the project? What will you use it for? How detailed and technical do you want it to be? What format would be best?' Ask if it's ok to revert later if you have more questions.

Sometimes (and entirely without malice), your manager may not have given sufficient thought to her request. She might be busy and distracted. In asking a few good questions, as well as helping her to clarify what she wants, you are improving your chances of giving her something she'll find useful. Provided you ask with genuine curiosity and not because you can't be bothered to think for yourself, asking questions can only help. Remember to take notes. You won't make the best impression by returning later to ask her to repeat herself.

Even if you've taken good notes, you might discover later that you need a bit more information or clarification. Anticipate this by asking your manager at the outset if you can come back to check you're on the right track. It may be that she's going to be out of the office for a few days and will tell you who to check with if she is going to be unreachable. Believe me, this will be far less stressful for you than having a problem, discovering that your manager isn't contactable and not knowing who to ask for help while your deadline ticks closer.

Timing

When does she need it? It is tempting to rush off and finish the task as soon as possible. But, depending on how much work is expected, 'as soon as possible' might be a week from now.

If your manager has asked for a two-page memo in ten days, you might produce a better-quality piece of work by getting an early night and putting in a few days' work instead of burning the midnight oil today to get it done in a fraction of that time. Would she like you to update her in a few days so she can see how your work is going? Don't forget to let your colleagues know if you are going to be out of the office, whether that's for vacation, training or otherwise.

Getting the simple things right

Attention to detail is important, so check your work for spelling or arithmetical errors. A simple mistake can undermine an otherwise excellent piece of work. It might help if you read aloud what you've written or even ask a colleague to have a quick look. Reread the notes you took initially and in any follow-up conversations. Are you providing what was requested?

Shortly after I started my first job in Dublin, the head of the division asked me to prepare a one-page schedule relating to the expenses of the tennis club where he was a member. The schedule was the same as that done previously, with one small exception: an extra expense needed to be included. It wasn't difficult, and I raced to get it done quickly, adding in a line to include the extra expense. It was only as I watched him add up the column of numbers that I realised I had forgotten to amend the formula for the total to reflect the extra expense line. Far from impressing him with my quick turnaround, I showed myself to be careless. It was not my best performance, and it was excruciatingly embarrassing.

Follow up

I'll talk more about getting feedback later but for now, it's a good idea to check in with your manager once she's had a chance to look at your work. Was it what she was expecting? Is there anything else you can do to help? If you feel she has time to answer and has had a chance to look at your work properly, you should also ask if there was *one* thing you could have done better. You may be surprised at how useful this quick feedback can be.

Prioritising

There is a balance to be struck between showing you're engaged and willing to work hard on the one hand and taking on too much on the other. With experience, you'll get better at gauging your workload, and it will help if you ask your manager how long she expects you to spend on various pieces of work. If you're concerned you have too much to do, ask your manager for help in prioritising your to-do list, there and then. Don't simply refuse the latest request.

Inevitably, though, you'll likely only realise you have too much on your to-do list when you've already agreed to do everything on it. First, take some comfort from Hofstadter's Law. This states that the time it takes to complete a project will always be longer than you expect, even if you account for Hofstadter's Law. In other words, even with the benefit of experience, we can all find ourselves in this position.

In these circumstances, you might be tempted to work as hard as you can and simply hope you'll get everything done in the agreed time. This approach carries a risk that you won't get everything done (or at least not done well), and by the time your manager realises you can't deliver, time has ticked by and there is less time for anyone else to help.

So how should you prioritise? The short answer is that there is no hard and fast rule. It's certainly not the case that tasks should automatically be prioritised based on the seniority of the person who made the request.

Communication is your saviour here. You should update your manager regularly on your progress, even if you believe you have everything under control. And if you think you may have a problem getting everything done, ask your manager for advice straightaway. She can help you to estimate how long tasks will take and to prioritise. You can then circle back to those colleagues whose work you don't expect to finish in the agreed timescale. Explain how you've come up with your plan and let them know when you're proposing to get their work done. It's key to remember that your primary responsibility is to communicate. Planning to work ridiculous hours and hoping that everything will magically get done is not a viable strategy. You run the risk of exhausting yourself and upsetting your manager and colleagues at the same time.

Remember ... when you're taking instruction at work ...

1. Take notes and ask questions to give yourself the best chance of delivering what is required.
2. Get the simple stuff right by checking your work before you hand it back.
3. Once your manager has had a chance to review your work, if you can, ask if there is one thing you could have done better.
4. If you have several things to do and you're not sure how to prioritise, or you realise you're unlikely to get everything done on time, ask for advice as soon as possible so that other colleagues can get involved if needed.

You've got this.
Love, Mum x

1.6 Having a growth mindset –
why 'I can't do that *yet*' is a good starting point, and why wanting to prove that you're right or that you're smart won't help you improve

Dear Joseph,

You've been in the new role for a couple of weeks now and you've been invited onto a proper project. It will make a pleasant change from the odd jobs you've been filling your days with so far. Although you're not entirely sure what you'll be doing, you are keen to get stuck in.

It's vital that you understand that there are skills that you don't have yet but that, with help from others and effort on your part, you can acquire. Carol Dweck, a professor at Stanford University, identified this approach as having a growth mindset.[18]

A growth mindset

A growth mindset is not merely having an open mind and a positive outlook or hoping for the best. Instead, it means believing that skills can be developed, and learning requires time and effort.

When faced with a new challenge taking you out of your comfort zone, with a growth mindset you would say, 'I've learnt new things before, and I can learn this new skill.' You would understand that mistakes are a learning opportunity.

---

18 *Mindset, the New Psychology of Success* by Carol Dweck.

'While I have not learnt this skill *yet*, I can work on it and get better.' You would recognise that basic ability is just the starting point for what can be achieved, so you can focus less on looking smart and more on learning and improving. I had the privilege of having some team members who had a growth mindset right from the very start. They were explicit about their desire to learn, and they asked lots of questions to understand (which often helped me clarify my thinking). They weren't defensive when they got something wrong or left an analysis incomplete. But they endeavoured not to make the same mistake twice. They were a pleasure to work with.

I had to have a growth mindset when I moved from Dublin to London. When I moved, I had experience in reading and analysing legal provisions, and there were lots of similarities between Irish and UK law. On the face of it, a move should not have been too onerous. But UK law was considerably more extensive; in analysing any specific issue, I couldn't be sure what other provisions might have been enacted or when. I didn't know what I didn't know. It was frustrating at times; I would think I had nailed some analysis based on the UK law that I knew about, only for my manager to ask if I had considered some changes that had been enacted at a different time in a separate piece of legislation. I had to accept that I had more to learn, believing I could improve with effort.

In writing this book, I also needed to stay in a growth mindset. Although I did my best in the early drafts, to give myself the best chance of writing a useful book, I needed to have input from people in the first 10–12 years of their career. I was fortunate to have a group of early readers who understood my goal and took the time to provide their perspectives and suggestions for improvement. Being defensive about what I had already written would have gotten me nowhere.

A fixed mindset

In contrast, if you had the (arguably more common) fixed mindset, you'd believe that skills and intelligence are predetermined and cannot be improved. With this view of the world, you either have a knack for something or you don't. Someone with a fixed mindset would do anything to avoid making a mistake and will have an irrational concern about being right and looking smart. These people will see challenges as roadblocks and think, *I'm not interested in this and I'm not good at it, so why waste time trying?*

Who likes to admit they're wrong or aren't sure what to do? I've never enjoyed it, and it's even harder when we are new to a team. After all, it's a time when we want to make the right impression. But make no mistake; bluffing will soon be found out. Instead of worrying about letting everyone down, including yourself, remember that it's easier for your colleagues to teach you when you admit that you need help.

Strategies you can use to improve or acquire a growth mindset

1. *Cultivate confident humility.*[19]

By taking the time to know your strengths and acknowledging that there will always be room for improvement, you'll see yourself as a work in progress. This kind of humility reflects confidence in your ability to learn and shows that you care more about improving yourself than proving yourself. There is a confidence sweet spot where you have faith in your capability while appreciating that you may not have the right skills *yet*. In this mindset, you have enough doubt to re-examine your existing knowledge and enough confidence to pursue new insights or ways of working.

---

19   See Adam Grant, *Think Again* at page 46 et seq.

Anya Hindmarch is an award-winning accessories designer and entrepreneur. In her book *If In Doubt, Wash Your Hair*, she points out that the more mountains you climb, the more confident you become. And the more confident you become, the bigger the mountain you can tackle next. I spent most of my twenties in abject fear of public speaking. I even turned down a few leadership roles because I knew the roles would involve giving presentations to large groups. Eventually, I asked for professional help to overcome my fear and become a better speaker. I learnt that remembering to breathe and preparing my content helps a great deal, a lesson I relied on when I gave my TEDx talk[20] (though if you listen closely, you can see I was still very nervous at the start).

The point is that if you keep proving to yourself that you can learn, you begin to trust yourself and you realise that often the only limitations are the barriers you impose on yourself. Hindmarch believes, and I agree, that you can do almost anything if you're determined enough.

2. ***Prioritise learning over getting approval.***
This is hard because we all like to hear that we are doing well. But prioritising approval over learning means we will want to minimise our mistakes by avoiding new things. When you show your more experienced colleagues that you are eager to learn, they will be more motivated to help you.

This is not the same as simply asking for help the moment you face a new challenge. That can just be lazy. Instead, reflect on what's being asked of you, come up with a plan, and then ask for input and guidance if you aren't confident in your approach. And when you've finished

---

20 *https://www.youtube.com/watch?v=CSy7XjXsvt4*

your task and received feedback, make it your primary goal to learn from that feedback. (See more on learning from feedback in *Part 3*.)

3. ***Choose to learn well over learning fast.***
   When you're asked to tackle a new area, remember it's more important to understand unfamiliar concepts and ideas than to convey as a quick answer something you don't really comprehend.

   Someone with a fixed mindset will want to reach the end goal as soon as possible. If they need to ask a question, they will focus on the answer they are given rather than understanding why the answer is what it is. They don't understand that this approach means they won't learn enough to solve a similar problem in the future. Someone with a growth mindset will take the time to understand the reasoning behind an answer and will be better equipped to deal with unexpected challenges in a similar area.

   While you will not set out to make mistakes, accept that because you are learning, they will happen and that's ok. Mistakes don't mean you are a failure. They just mean that you have not acquired the necessary skills yet. But, by trying, you're on the right track.

4. ***Learn from the mistakes of others.***
   While it's unhealthy to compare yourself to others, when you see someone else make a mistake, remember it so that when you are in a similar situation, you can apply that lesson. For example, you might observe that how your colleague handled a situation made it worse, and you can appreciate the alternative steps that might have helped.

   In the same vein, when you're faced with a new challenge, remember that it's likely someone else has faced something similar. It can be helpful to sense-check your plan with some colleagues. They may very well have some helpful experiences to share.

5. ***Cultivate the ability to stick to long-term goals and to keep going despite adversity.***
   Angela Duckworth has found that grit, a combination of passion and perseverance for a singularly important goal is the hallmark of high achievers in every domain.[21] You can assess your level of grit using her scale at *https:// angeladuckworth.com/grit-scale/*

Remember ... to build a growth mindset ...

1. Cultivate confident humility. Start with simply taking a pause when you're taken outside your comfort zone. Although this is a new challenge, consider the real possibility that you can and will learn how to do this well.
2. Show that you are keen to learn by doing as much as you can yourself and asking for help when you're not sure.
3. Remind yourself you've done difficult things in the past and you can learn new things that are difficult.
4. It's more important to improve yourself than to prove yourself.

You've got this.
Love, Mum x

---

21 Angela Duckworth, *Grit*

1.7 How it's easy to be misunderstood

Dear Joseph,

It took me a long time to appreciate that a colleague and I could see the same facts in different ways, and I wish I'd known earlier how easily this can happen.

Impact vs intention

Imagine that you are in a team meeting. You're excited to be on the project, albeit as the most junior person you seem to have responsibility for the boring admin jobs. The meeting is ending, and you're given another dull task to add to your to-do list. Because you want to get these tasks finished as soon as possible, you leave the meeting abruptly without chatting to your colleagues. You believe your speedy getaway shows you to be hardworking and efficient, but others see you as brusque at best, sullen at worst. Suddenly you don't seem like such a team player after all. In other situations, you may consider yourself shy, but others can see you as aloof. Or you prize your truth-telling, but others see you as brutal and unfeeling.

It's human nature to judge our own actions by our intentions. But we judge others by their impact on us, not least because we usually don't know their intentions. Remember that your development depends, among other things, on how well you work with others. So, how your colleagues feel – that is, the impact you've had on them – matters, and you need to know. In future, you might want to say something that could help them understand your intentions. 'Wow, I've got a lot to do. I'd better get cracking. See you later.' I'll mention this a lot: clear communication is very important. (See also *Part 4, Preparing to have a difficult conversation*.)

Attribution

Another reason why we sometimes don't see things the way others see them is because we tend to attribute our own actions to the situation, but we attribute others' actions to their character. Perhaps you turned up late to a meeting because you were busy finishing off something for another manager. In your mind, it was the work deadline which made you late. But your colleagues see you arrive late and conclude you are unreliable or rude.

Traits

And there is a third reason why we often see things differently from others. When we show any kind of emotion that we aren't proud of, say, impatience or anger, we like to think of it as a rare event. If the behaviour is pointed out to us, we comfort ourselves that that trait is not really who we are. We subtract our emotions. But others see it and count it twice. 'She is always bad-tempered.'

Hopefully understanding how all of us interpret behaviours will help you appreciate that you may not come across to your colleagues as you intend.

Remember ... it's easy to be misunderstood because ...

1. Our actions may have a different impact to what we intended.
2. We all tend to attribute others' actions to their character, rather than to the situation.
3. Although we forgive ourselves for occasional missteps, we tend to 'double count' others for theirs.

You've got this.
Love, Mum x

PART 2
Communication Skills

2.1 Sending and receiving emails
– some basic etiquette and why you should often resist the temptation to reach for the keyboard

Dear Joseph,

It's inevitable that you will conduct a decent proportion of your work by email and/or other messaging apps that don't involve voice or in-person interaction.

You'll learn some email etiquette from observing others in your work environment and, in any event, norms change over time so some of what I write here may be out of date when you're reading this.

Sending emails

Some tips:
- If you've received a request by email, don't leave the sender guessing if and when you might respond. One of the most common problems with email communications arises because of a delay in responding. So, send a holding email while you think about it. E.g., 'Let me check this with Matt and I'll get back to you by tomorrow. If you need an answer quickly, please let me know.' Or 'Jane is in the Far East so it might take me a while to get an answer from her.'
- If you're a recipient of a group email, be careful you don't respond by 'Reply All'. And when you're sending an email to more than one recipient, it's a good idea to read out loud the names in the to, cc and bcc boxes. It's too easy,

especially with autofill, to find an email address included in error. Better to check twice and send once, with no need for apologies or attempting to recall an email. Often, the recall function simply highlights the error without rectifying it so it's best to avoid needing to use it.

- In general, it's better to err on the side of formality than risk being seen as unprofessional. Use proper punctuation and full words. Do not be tempted to use acronyms or slang unless you are replying to someone who has used them in their emails to you. (This is similar to the matching technique described in *Part 1, Building rapport*.)

- Emojis can also look too casual in a professional context so use them judiciously. I know we often use emojis to illustrate our intention in private messages and they can be helpful, provided they are interpreted in the same way as the sender intended. You may want to send a smiley face to show that you're being friendly, but the recipient could think that you are indifferent to the pressure they're under.

- Aim to use clear language and be as brief as you can. In 1657, Blaise Pascal, a famous mathematician, inventor and philosopher, published a collection of open letters and within them noted 'I have made this longer than usual because I have not had time to make it shorter.' Brevity takes time but it's worth the effort to make your communication easier to read by the recipient. It's so easy to compose an email as if we were talking to the recipient, but we use far more words in speech than we need to convey our point effectively in writing. If I need to send an email, I usually draft it and leave it for an hour or so. With a fresh eye, it's easier to edit before I send it.

- If you need to convey a lot of information, you can use bold/ underlining for subheadings or to emphasise key messages. Numbered paragraphs or bullet points will make it easier for the recipient to refer to what you've said if they need to respond or raise a query.

- If you're asking for a quick answer from the recipient, let them know if you are not going to be at your desk or online for a while. That way, they won't get frustrated trying to get hold of you when you've gone out to buy a sandwich.

Sending 'difficult' emails

Sometimes, you may need to send an email that would involve a difficult conversation if you were dealing with the recipient in person. (More on difficult conversations in *Part 4*.) A difficult email might be one where you need to give information that you know the recipient won't like, e.g., a deadline will be missed, costs will be greater than estimated, or a valued team member is no longer available to work on a project.

In these circumstances, you need to bear in mind that an email exchange is not a dialogue. It is a serial monologue because there's no opportunity to interrupt for clarification. And we can't adjust our behaviour as we go based on the other person's reaction because we can't see their facial expression and body language. It's also not easy to test our assumptions about the other person's intentions. Research shows that an in-person request is more than thirty times more successful than a request that has been emailed.[22]

If you believe the recipient is going to react badly to the substance of your email, consider going to see them or having a conversation in preference to sending an email. Seeing them in person is better than a video call, which in turn is better than a simple phone call, which beats an email. Even if you will need to follow up with a confirmatory email providing

---

22   *https://hbr.org/2017/04/a-face-to-face-request-is-34-times-more-successful-than-an-email*

more detail, your chances of handling the relationship well are increased by having a conversation first by whatever medium is available.

But if in-person communication is not possible, you'll want to draft the email so that it's effective in delivering your message while minimising the risks of making the situation worse. It might be that you need to chase a colleague who is not responding to your requests for help, or you are seeking clarification from a client who seems to have changed what they're asking for.

To reduce the risk of being misunderstood, go out of your way to explain yourself. For example, 'I'm asking about the timing on this because I know my manager will ask soon. She promised the report would be sent to the client yesterday.' Or you might email a client seeking clarification, 'I'm asking because I'm not entirely clear and I don't want to waste time.'

The fact is, in the cold light of day, an email that we intended to be brief, friendly and informative can be perceived as curt, disrespectful and presumptive. If you've been as explicit as you can be, but you aren't sure you're getting the tone right, ask someone else to read the draft before you send it. The answer will rarely be to write more; usually, a different word here and there is enough to achieve the tone you want.

Responding to emails you've received that evoke a negative response

It's not easy to be the recipient of a difficult email either. Once you've read an email that provokes a negative reaction, you will automatically start to make assumptions about the sender's intentions. This is entirely natural; we make sense of our world by telling ourselves a story about what happens. And when we are tired or stressed, that story is likely to be more negative. But you need to remind yourself that you cannot know the sender's intentions. Their intentions could be positive, mixed, negative, or they may have no particular intentions in connection with you at all. They may be focused on something or someone else entirely and have dashed off an email to you without thinking through how you might interpret it.

To get a more balanced view of the contents, Simon Collins, a senior figure in the City, recommends reading a difficult email three times: the first time in as neutral a voice as possible, the second as if it's from a person who is on your side and is trying to be helpful, and (if necessary) a third time in a cartoon voice. I've done this and it definitely takes the heat out of my reaction.

There is also wisdom in the advice to sleep on it. In his book *Thinking, Fast and Slow*, Daniel Kahneman describes two systems of thinking. System 1 is fast, intuitive and emotional, while System 2 is slower, more deliberative and logical. Allowing yourself to sleep on it can help leverage System 2's ability to process information more thoroughly and make a more informed decision.

Whatever you do, don't send off a quick response. Instead, when your emotions have settled, ideally talk to the person. It is simply too difficult to resolve a conflict over email with another email. There is too big a risk that anything you write can exacerbate the situation. Although you might be nervous about approaching the sender of a curt message, most people are generally less cranky in person than they might appear from an email. Take seriously the possibility that there's something important you don't know so you can make it easier for them to tell you what they think. (See more about having difficult conversations in *Part 4*.)

As you know, Joseph, we've had a long-standing relationship with a local taxi driver. Some time ago, she emailed me about increasing her rates. I responded to say I was concerned about how expensive trips might become. In her answer, she set out the details of her proposal and ended her email with this: 'Thank you for your kind attention. My command of English may not come across very well when I set out information in an email. Please do not feel in any way that I am being anything but friendly. My husband says I can be too matter-of-fact and can be misunderstood as aggressive. I don't mean to be.' It was a perfect ending because, until then, I thought the exchange had been a bit terse. We came to a happy compromise, and all was well. My point here is that, to preserve our relationship at a time when she was delivering an unwanted message, this lady made an extra effort in communicating with me. I appreciated her effort, and the relationship was in fact improved, not harmed, by the exchange.

Remember ... when you're sending emails ...

1. Silence isn't golden: if you've received a request by email, acknowledge it and indicate when you'll be able to answer it if you can't do so straightaway.
2. Take the time to draft an email so that it's as clear and concise as possible. Your first attempt will almost certainly need some editing.
3. It's very challenging if not impossible to resolve difficult issues by email. If you can't communicate with your correspondent in person, ask someone else to read your draft response before you send it to check the tone. In the hierarchy of communication, in-person beats videocall, which is better than a phone call, which is preferable to an email.
4. If you've received a 'difficult' email, don't assume you know what the sender's intentions were, and don't respond immediately.

You've got this.
Love, Mum x

2.2 Listening – some techniques to help you understand someone else's message

Dear Joseph,

Research has shown that good listeners have deeper interpersonal bonds and produce better results. They give respect and gain insight.[23] To live up to your potential at work, you need to be a good listener, whether you're understanding what is being asked of you or dealing with difficult issues within your team or with your clients. Crossed wires or tension in the workplace can come about because we don't understand our colleagues' perspectives, and that's usually because we haven't listened well enough. Whether you realise it or not, you will need good listening skills from your first day.

Does your colleague want support or input?

Let's say a colleague is struggling with a work issue, and they want to talk to you about it. The first thing you need to understand is whether your colleague is looking for your support or your input. If your colleague is emotional, they're more likely to be looking for support, at least in the first instance. And if they're looking for potential solutions to a

---

23   Adam Grant is a bestselling author and professor at the Wharton School of the University of Pennsylvania specialising in organisational psychology. I heartily recommend all of his books. He tweeted about this research on 18 November 2024.

problem, they'll usually make that clear. If you're not sure, you can ask your colleague how they would like you to help.

The competing monologue in your head can make it hard to listen

A barrier to listening can be our own emotions, where our sensitivities keep our minds busy. (*I cannot believe she is complaining about having too much work. I'd give anything to be on that project. It's way more interesting than what I'm doing.*) When I was a junior, I often had a commentary in my head: *I can't believe you're asking me to do [that task]. I didn't need to go to university for this*! Whatever it is, our emotions can distract us from paying attention to what the other person is saying.

And sometimes, the other person's emotions can make it difficult to know how to respond. Your colleagues are human, so they're going to get stressed and upset. In those situations, I've found myself pretending to listen while waiting for the other person to breathe so I can interrupt them to give my perspective.

But these internal conversations and the desire to put across our own viewpoint do nothing to help us understand what is going on with the other person.

It's ok not to have an answer …

Bear in mind that smart people are often worse listeners because they identify more issues and are more likely to assume that they already know what the other person is going to say. Whether the other person wants support or input, it's better to concentrate on asking questions to understand without leaping to solutions.

The poet John Keats believed that to be a person of achievement, one must have 'negative capability', which he described as 'capable of being in uncertainties … doubts, without any irritable reaching after fact and reason'. He was not using the word 'negative' in a pejorative sense. Instead, his belief was that a person's potential can be defined by their ability to be comfortable with uncertainty and ambiguity, without fixating on immediate answers and conclusions. If you can listen without rehearsing your next sentence, you'll learn more and make a better contribution.

And remember that, usually, when someone is emotional about a difficult situation, they don't expect a magic response that will fix everything. If there were simple answers, they would likely have thought of them. In sharing their difficulty, your colleague wants to be understood and to feel they are not alone in solving the problem. So, it's ok to simply say, 'I don't know what to say. It's a tough situation.'

... but sympathy is not the best response

Even if we've listened, our response can shut down the conversation if we try to sympathise. Sympathy is when you commiserate with or pity someone else who is experiencing misfortune. But sympathy drives disconnection because it creates an uneven power dynamic (*it's happening to you, not me*), and it can lead to more isolation for the speaker. 'That sounds so awful. Poor you.'

When someone is emotional,

- try to show empathy

Empathy is the ability to share someone else's feelings or experiences by imagining what it would be like to be *that person* in *that situation*. To do that:

- try to understand their perspective and accept that that's how things seem to them. Ask questions to understand.

'How do you feel about this?' 'Tell me more about that.'
'How did that happen?'

- acknowledge how they're feeling ('That sounds overwhelming.') without suggesting how you would feel in their shoes. If you've misunderstood, your colleague will likely correct you. 'No, it's more like frustration.'
- imagine how it feels when you experience that emotion (even if these circumstances wouldn't evoke that emotion for you).
- resist being judgemental about the appropriateness of their feelings. I find this hard sometimes, and I have to remind myself that my judgement won't help me understand their perspective.

- and avoid

- telling a story about something similar happening to you. This is not about you.
- minimising their concerns or finding a silver lining. This invalidates how the other person feels and drives disconnection. Often, we offer platitudes because we find it uncomfortable to watch someone else in distress, and it makes us feel better.
- asking incidental questions. They disrupt the other person's train of thought. We once had a neighbour who would often interrupt his wife's stories to confirm some incidental detail. For example, Jane would describe a funny incident on the high street. She'd be building up to her punchline when Norman would interrupt to ask exactly where on the high street she'd been at the time. In her story, the precise location was completely irrelevant. We were interested in what happened and how it felt. You will remember in our house that 'Doing a Norman' became synonymous with this type of conversational contribution.

Some fun facts about listening

Good listening usually involves some silence. If you fill the silence too soon, you can prevent the speaker from saying what they need to say. Instead of offering an opinion or asking a question, you can pause for a few seconds, which may be enough for them to say more. And you can encourage them with phrases like 'Tell me more.'

Research has found that language comprehension is generally better and faster if you listen through your right ear because what is heard in the right ear is routed first to the left side of the brain. The left ear may be better at recognising the emotional aspects of speech as well as appreciating music and poetry.[24]

Remember ... when you're listening ...

1. You should be listening *to understand*, so focus on the speaker and their concerns and feelings.
2. Figure out if your colleague wants support or input. If they're emotional, usually they'll want support, at least in the first instance. Try to be empathic (not sympathetic), and avoid offering quick fixes or platitudes.
3. If you catch yourself diagnosing, advising or reassuring your colleague, pause and get back to listening to understand.[25]

You've got this.
Love, Mum x

---

24 Right ear for comprehension – *https://pmc.ncbi.nlm.nih.gov/articles/PMC8295541/*
Left ear for emotional recognition – *https://pubmed.ncbi.nlm.nih.gov/23461765/*
Left ear for music/ poetry appreciation – *https://journals.sagepub.com/doi/10.1177/10298649221126904?icid=int.sj-abstract.citing-articles.6*

25 More on this in *People Skills* by Robert Bolton, a very practical guide to communication at work and outside it.

2.3 Persuasion – how to work with others to change their mind or help you to recognise when it's time to change your mind

Dear Joseph,

Sometimes, you will want to persuade someone to do something different. In such circumstances, all of us would like to simply change the other's mind so they agree with us.

Unfortunately, no one can change your mind except you. And the same goes for the other person. The best you can hope for is that you can persuade them to think again, to contemplate the possibility that they could reconsider.

But let's face it. Hearing the same thing over and over is just boring for the other person. And if they don't feel you're interested in their viewpoint, they're more likely to become entrenched in it than change it.

Understanding the other's position

To get off on the right foot, first you need to listen and understand *why* they think what they think. Trying to persuade them to think differently without understanding their perspective is like trying to make an omelette without breaking eggs. So, ask lots of questions, not in an aggressive or badgering way but from curiosity. Who knows! It may be that *they* will persuade *you* to change your mind. (If you haven't read the last letter on listening, I recommend you do that before you read the rest of this letter.)

Ask the person how they came to their viewpoint. What happened to convince them? What would they need to see before they would contemplate changing their mind? 'If I wanted you to rethink this, how should I go about it?' As you talk about the issues, acknowledge that the other person has the freedom to choose their opinion. 'I know I might not be able to persuade you to think differently. I would like to make sure, though, that we understand each other.'

It's helpful to acknowledge where your respective views overlap. This doesn't make you weaker. It shows you are willing to acknowledge areas of common understanding and you're not just trying to make the other person wrong. A close friend of mine was once frustrated in his discussions with a peer about how to organise their team. He felt the discussion had become a battle of wills between their respective viewpoints. But he managed to change the atmosphere by acknowledging that they had a common goal; they both wanted the best for their customers. He asked his colleague if they could start the discussion again, this time from the viewpoint of the customers who would be impacted by any organisational changes. That simple but explicit acknowledgement of a common goal and a shift to the perspective of their customers took the heat out of the discussion, and they were able to agree on a way forward.

Let's say you are trying to persuade someone to help you, for example, a co-worker whose input you need, or a hotel receptionist at check-in, and they won't engage with you on your issue. Frustrated, you might be tempted to lose your temper and speak that little bit louder. But that approach rarely works. One way of unlocking the stalemate can be to ask them what they would do in your position. Inviting someone to be in your shoes can evoke enough empathy for them to help or at least advise you on how to accomplish your objective.

Be clear about what would be involved for the other person if you succeed in persuading them to change

When you're trying to persuade someone to do something different, take the time to understand what it would mean for them to change what they are doing already. Even if they're convinced of the benefits of your proposal, the cost to them may be enough to prevent them from acting differently.

In one of my earliest leadership positions, I led a team who advised a range of investors in commercial real estate, investing in assets like offices, hotels and warehouses. I wanted to change how we organised ourselves and interacted with our clients. I set out a vision of a new way of working where we would each have clients from no more than two investor classes. This concentration of industry knowledge would enable us to build communities of like-minded investors, benefitting our clients and therefore us too. I have to admit I was pretty pleased with myself when my colleagues agreed that the new model would be an improvement.

However, that warm feeling soon faded when I realised that although everyone seemed to appreciate the benefits of a different model, a few colleagues steadfastly refused to change how they operated. I eventually realised that changing to the new model would require them to give up something that was important to them. Specifically, the new model would require them to transfer some of their existing client accounts to other colleagues. This would mean relinquishing relationships that had taken years to build and then building relationships with new clients with whom they had no guarantee of success. Understandably, they were reluctant to do that. I had focused solely on persuading my colleagues of the benefits of a result, and I hadn't considered that the journey to get there would be more painful for some of them. I should have thought about that before assuming everyone would simply move ahead with the reorganisation.

Storytelling

Storytelling is a powerful communication tool because we all make sense of our world by the stories we tell ourselves about it. I've used stories in some of these letters to illustrate why we behave the way we do, and how we might improve our interactions. In the same way, when you're trying to persuade someone to think again, using a story to illustrate your position can be helpful. The story can be something that has happened already, or a story about what could happen if something changed. Either way, evoking emotions in the other person can be helpful in persuading them to reconsider.

Avoid using a barrage of arguments

Try not to put forward lots of arguments for the other person to change their mind. Some of your arguments are bound to be weaker than others. Listing them all gives the other person the ability to pick the weakest argument and use that as the reason for sticking to their guns.

But that doesn't mean that you pick your killer argument and make it out to be perfect. Most issues are not black and white; they're complex and nuanced. You're more likely to get your colleague to reconsider if you can admit that your position has some caveats, and it's not consistent across all possibilities.

Stay good-humoured and curious

Don't let the debate become personal. It may be that you're more junior and feel that your more senior colleague isn't open to your viewpoint. Towards the end of my career in the advisory firm, I worked with a long-standing and more senior colleague. I was trying to persuade him on an issue, but I felt he still saw me as a junior, even though by that stage I'd had decades of experience. It didn't help that in my (relative) youth, I had had a reputation of jumping to conclusions, and I realised that he assumed I was still doing that. It was frustrating.

So, I stopped trying to persuade him of the advantages of my proposal for a few minutes. I acknowledged that while I had earned a 'shoot from the hip' reputation in the past, I had worked hard to become more considered. I asked him if he would think about 'updating his operating software' insofar as it related to me. He laughed and agreed that I wasn't a new graduate anymore and had more experience in this area than he did. He didn't agree to everything I proposed, but after this conversational detour, he was more open to reconsidering his position.

Persuading someone to change doesn't mean they have to admit they were wrong or misguided. Be generous and gracious when you've persuaded someone to think again. Don't demand their explicit acknowledgement that you were right and they were wrong.

Sometimes, persuasion seems impossible

Some people can be very reluctant to be persuaded to change their view. Adam Grant suggests that some traits make this behaviour likely.[26] In such cases, you might have to have several conversations before you make any progress.

1. *Arrogance*

Someone's overconfidence that they know it all can be the first barrier to changing their mind. Ask questions to show you're trying to understand and reflect out loud on their explanation. 'So, what I hear is that some of your clients would prefer to stay working with you and not transition to the new model. Does that mean the rest of the team

---

26 *https://hbr.org/2021/03/persuading-the-unpersuadable*

would have to remain the same too?' Reflecting on the implications of their position can provide an opportunity to broaden the discussion.

2. *Stubbornness*

Some people see consistency and certainty as virtues and believe that outcomes can be influenced by their willpower. When another person tries hard to change their mind, they snap back like a rubber band. Try asking questions like 'What if?' or 'Could we ...?' and to overcome their defensiveness, ask how small changes might work. Remember that your objective is to have them reconsider their position, and even a small change can be a start.

3. *Narcissism*

People who are narcissistic believe they're special and superior, and they can be hostile if they think that they or their ideas are being insulted or rejected. One approach is to praise the person in an area adjacent to the one where you are trying to change their minds. Let's imagine your colleague holds a strong and contrary view on a staff issue. Perhaps acknowledge how good she is at training her team before trying to persuade her of your viewpoint. I don't generally use compliments to get my way, not least because people who are self-aware are wary of flattery. But for those who appear to consistently believe they're special and won't listen, a sincere compliment can be disarming.

4. *Disagreeableness*

People who are argumentative and appear as if they are trying to crush debate can seem disagreeable and scary. But often their behaviour belies the fact that they are energised by conflict, and they enjoy having a debate with someone who doesn't agree straightaway. An Irish friend of mine (who I don't think is disagreeable at all) will argue her position on an issue vociferously but will then listen carefully to and reflect on the opposing view *if* the other person has been brave enough to stick around. In the same vein, a story circulated on Reddit some years ago that at Apple, there was an unofficial award given to one person every year who had had the guts to challenge Steve Jobs. Apparently, Jobs was aware of it and liked the idea. So, don't just give in. Try using some of the tips above.

Remember ... when you're trying to persuade someone to think differently ...

1. Curiosity is your friend. Work hard to understand why your colleague thinks as they do. Ask questions to understand (not to badger the other person).
2. Thinking in terms of right and wrong is not likely to help you achieve change. Be proactive in pointing out the weaknesses in your own argument, and explicitly acknowledge areas of agreement.
3. Use stories to illustrate your point, and stay good-humoured.
4. If you expect a colleague to be difficult to persuade, take the time to prepare your approach and accept that you might have to have several conversations.

You've got this.
Love, Mum x

2.4 Delegating – some tips to help get the job done

Dear Joseph,

After some time (a few months in some roles, longer in others), you will likely be expected to delegate work to others so that, together, you can complete larger projects.

Delegation can bring numerous benefits. It allows you to concentrate on tasks that better suit your skillset or experience so that, overall, the team's efficiency is boosted. It can also give you the space to learn something new. At the same time, entrusting that task to someone less senior gives that person the opportunity to develop their skills and to increase their visibility, whether that's within the organisation or externally.

But delegation is not abdication; delegated work becomes a shared task, and you will need to stay involved to offer help and share responsibility. It takes skill to delegate, so you may make mistakes before you learn how to do it well.

What to delegate?

Before you start the delegation conversation with your colleague, pause to reflect on *what* you want to delegate. Do you have a clear idea of what needs to be done? How would you go about this task if you were going to do it yourself? How long do you think it will take? Remember that we often underestimate the time it will take to do something. (More on this in *Part 1, Taking instruction and prioritising tasks*.) Will your colleague need input from anyone else? Are you expecting a written report or summary to be produced? What form should it take? Who will read it, internally and externally? A common cause of disappointment with delegated work is the lack of clarity around what was required. Delegating thoughtlessly is just dumping on someone else. If you do that, you don't deserve and shouldn't expect a good outcome.

Be prepared to explain the context within which this work will be done and why you would approach it in the way you suggest. We all make sense of the world through stories. Even if, say, the more junior person will have no opportunity to meet the customer who is paying for this work, they will feel more involved in the project if you take a few minutes to explain why this work is necessary. It's even better if you can share a few anecdotes to bring the wider project to life. Context is important because, in sharing this, you are also giving your colleague the opportunity to offer their thoughts on how the task might be accomplished. You never know; they might come up with a better way. And if you think you may need to refine your request as more information becomes available, let your colleague know that upfront.

Bear in mind that if you delegate too much, you will likely become too far removed from the work being done and fail to realise when your junior colleagues need more support. Not only can this lead to missed deadlines, but it is also stressful for your colleagues, whose confidence may be crushed when the project goes badly.

To whom?

Ideally, you will have an opportunity to work with someone on low- stakes, non-urgent work before you must hand over time-sensitive and complex work. As you build the relationship with your colleague, explain that quick wins on easy tasks build trust, making it easier for you to delegate larger, more complex responsibilities later. (See also *Part 1, Earning trust.*)

Do you expect your junior colleague to know how to do this work already? Whatever your expectations, you should discuss them to avoid frustration and disappointment for both of you. Consider what kind of support and frequency of check-in you would like in their place and ask them what they might like. If the junior colleague is not very experienced in this sort of work, you should schedule regular, appropriately spaced check-ins to keep progress on track. Leave it too late to check in, and an impending deadline can increase stress levels for everyone. Lastly, don't forget that training a more junior colleague will help you look good too.

The golden rule of delegating

In the nuts and bolts of delegation, there is no more appropriate advice to bear in mind than the golden rule: 'treat others as you'd like to be treated yourself'. Go back to the letter in *Part 1, Taking instructions and prioritising tasks*. What would you want to know if you were asked to complete these tasks? You'd likely prefer to have a conversation where you are given the context of the request and the opportunity to ask questions than receiving an email setting out a to-do list.

And delegating involves more than dishing out instructions and checking in occasionally. You will need to teach and coach less experienced colleagues if they are to develop.

I remember a senior colleague asking me to research a particular issue and draft a letter of advice to the client. There was no urgency so I decided to get a more junior colleague involved so we could both learn. We spent a bit of time making sure we'd covered all the points and took the draft advice note to our boss. He put it to one side and said, without apologising or giving a reason, 'Oh, I decided to write that myself and sent it to the client three days ago.' We were furious; he hadn't even given us a copy of his advice so we could see if our analysis was right.

As you work together, show appreciation for your colleague's efforts, say thank you and check in on how they're getting on more generally. Your colleague has professional aspirations and a personal life just like you, so don't treat them merely as a vehicle to make your life easier. They deserve your respect. If, during the project, you develop your thinking so that you 'move the goalposts' and ask for something different, explain why you've done that. You will only build resentment if you pretend otherwise.

When the delegated tasks are complete, make time to reflect with your colleague on how it went. Ask for their take on it and see if they have any suggestions on how it could be done better next time. Offer feedback on how they might improve. If things get tense, you might want to check out the letters in *Part 4, Difficult conversations* (and especially the parts about blame and contribution).

TEACH

Here's an acronym that summarises the rest of this letter and might help you delegate well:

Trust – you'll need to trust the person you're delegating to, and they will need to trust that you have their back. And trust takes effort. (If you haven't read it already, see *Earning Trust in Part 1*.)

Explain – take the time to explain the details of what's involved as well as the context. Is this part of a larger project? In what form do you want your colleague to present their work? What is the timing?

Audience – who will use or benefit from this work and for what purpose? Sharing this with your colleagues will help them help you.

Coach – to delegate well, you'll need to check in with your colleagues, providing support and advice to help them learn.

How to do it better – after the job is done, make time to reflect with your colleague on how it went. Don't forget this discussion is a two-way street. Give feedback to your colleagues on their performance, but also ask how you could have done a better job delegating. Learning should be everyone's aim.

What's stopping you from delegating?

It might be that you've had feedback that you don't delegate enough, or in the middle of doing a task, you realise that someone else should be doing it instead of you. A tell-tale sign that we're not delegating enough or not delegating well is that we're working long hours, but our junior colleagues are leaving on time, and they don't appear to be very engaged with our project.

Doing it all yourself carries a real cost. When this happened to me, I found myself overwhelmed, and my judgement and the quality of my work fell. And there was a cost to my colleagues' development, the team's efficiency and overall morale.

But sometimes, delegation itself feels like just another job, and you might conclude that it would take less time and effort to simply do it yourself. This often happens when a colleague needs more detailed instructions upfront and ongoing support than we want or believe we have time to give. Perhaps they've never undertaken a task like this one, and they need to learn the ropes.

It may not be the teaching part that stops delegation. We might have a streak of perfectionism and think we'll do a better job than someone else. Maybe we feel that if we let someone else in on 'our patch', our client or our boss might think we aren't so important anymore. Or we're insecure and afraid that a more junior person might do a better job than we would.

While these are understandable reasons for doing the work ourselves, they aren't good reasons. If, on reflection, you think you are falling into any of these traps and you're struggling to behave differently, seek guidance from a more experienced team member or a coach. Delegating is a skill like any other, and if you're struggling with it, accept that you have more to learn. You just can't do it well *yet*. (See *Part 1, Having a growth mindset*.)

Don't feel bad about this. Lots of people struggle with delegation, and asking for help to do the right thing is a strength. It's those who don't try to improve who are the weak links.

But if you've done your best to delegate and your colleague seems unable or unwilling to help, it might be time to have a conversation about the reasons for this. In those circumstances, check out *Part 4, Having difficult conversations*.

Remember ... if you are delegating ...

1. Treat your junior colleague as you would like to be treated in their shoes. Say please and thank you; stay close enough that you can appreciate their efforts and the challenges they face.

2. Remember to **TEACH** – build **t**rust, **e**xplain what's involved, identify the **a**udience for the work, **c**oach your colleague throughout the project and, at the end, reflect on **h**ow it could have gone better.

3. Be sincere in offering ongoing support so that your colleague knows this is a shared task; you aren't leaving them to it without support.

4. If you find delegating difficult, it is worth seeking advice on how to improve. An inability to delegate well can become a limiting factor to career progression.

You've got this.
Love, Mum x

PART 3
Developing Yourself and Working with Feedback

3.1 Everyone else has got it all figured out (or have they?) and having imposter syndrome

Dear Joseph,

Whether we admit it or not, most of us have looked around the workplace, mulling over our shortcomings and musing that our colleagues seem to find things easier. Not for them the tossing and turning in the small hours of the morning, rerunning a conversation or project that didn't go as they'd hoped. We imagine they have no insecurities; they appear confident and *if* they have development areas, we conclude that those must be considered minor by them and by senior colleagues. This harsh comparison is even more likely when we don't work closely with our peers. At best, we observe their interactions at a distance, where we cannot see their shortcomings and imagine there aren't any.

Apart from torturing ourselves that, somehow, we aren't good enough (see more on imposter syndrome below), there is a real disadvantage to believing that everyone else has got it all figured out. That belief can stop us from asking for help, as we don't want to appear weak, needy or incompetent by comparison. And if we don't ask for help when we need it, we make our lives much harder.

Does everyone else have it all figured out?

In the early years of my career, I knew from discussions with my close friends that although they appeared confident at work, they had work-related worries. But was this the case for just a few of us?

Years later, I began to coach high-performing less senior individuals who, if I'd been their peer, would have appeared to me to have had it all figured out. Sure, occasionally, they might have admitted publicly to having something to work on, but it wasn't something that seemed to dent their confidence. But appearances are deceiving and as I had conversations with these high performers, I found that these people were just like my friends and me. They too worried that they weren't good enough at one thing or another, and they also thought that *their* peers had everything figured out. It showed me that almost everyone has insecurities. Others don't have everything figured out, no matter how confident they appear. Instead of wasting energy in fruitless comparisons, it's much better to spend the time and effort on addressing whatever development areas you have.

Finally, there do seem to be a few people who really *are* super-confident with no insecurities, but I believe they have another more limiting issue – a lack of self-awareness. To be human is to be imperfect, so *everyone* has flaws. But to recognise these flaws in oneself requires some self-awareness. In any part of life which requires us to build relationships with others, I doubt there are many more limiting failings than a lack of self-awareness. As William Shakespeare wrote, 'The fool doth think he is wise, but the wise man knows himself to be a fool.'

Imposter syndrome

Imposter syndrome is where we experience self-doubt even in areas where we usually excel. It can haunt us if we have perfectionist tendencies, so that nothing less than consistent perfection is good enough. The Oxford Dictionary defines imposter syndrome as, 'the persistent inability to believe that one's success is deserved or has been legitimately achieved as a result of one's own efforts or skills'. This phenomenon feels like nervousness and accompanies a narrative in our head along the lines of: *Is today the day they're going to find me out*? Because it holds us back from enjoying the self-confidence we should feel given our accomplishments, it can affect how we approach projects or relationships. Then, if we behave as though our previous successes were flukes and we don't really know what we're doing, it can become a self-fulfilling prophecy; others see our hesitancy and begin to doubt us.

I am familiar with this feeling, and not only from my early career but throughout it; in fact, every time I took on a new role or challenge, I worried that others' faith in me was misplaced. It wasn't that I didn't want to learn; I just didn't believe I could ever be as effective as others seemed to believe. My previous successes were down to something or someone else. That voice was there as I prepared to give my TEDx talk about teams making strategic decisions. Despite my experience in just that area, I couldn't stop the voice in my head asking me what I thought I could possibly offer the audience. And I've been surprised how many objectively successful friends and colleagues have admitted they too suffer from this.

But there are advantages to having imposter syndrome. Provided it isn't debilitating, imposter syndrome can motivate us to work harder and pursue improvement. I estimate I practised my TEDx talk at least 100 times before I gave it. And those of us who suffer from imposter syndrome are often better learners; because we believe we have more to learn, we are more open to feedback and insight from others.

But sometimes these imposter thoughts are draining, even debilitating. I exhausted myself, listing all the ways I needed to do better and be better before I could be worthy of the good opinion in which others held me. At that point

I was fortunate to benefit from the support of a good coach, support I'd recommend if you find your imposter syndrome paralysing. She helped me see that although I didn't always believe in myself, senior colleagues whose opinion I valued *did* believe in me. And yet, in relation to my capabilities, I chose to believe myself, not them. Even I could appreciate the inherent contradiction that I trusted their opinion on everything professional, but not in relation to my capabilities. While I thought these colleagues were overestimating me, wasn't it possible I was underestimating myself? Maybe, with their experience, they could appreciate skills in me that I couldn't see in myself. I can't say this perspective cured me of my imposter syndrome, but remembering it did help me to avoid paralysis.

Remember ... when you think everyone else has 'got it all figured out' ... and it's just a matter of time before you're found out ...

1. Almost everyone compares themselves unfavourably to others, so try to be kinder to yourself, as you would to a friend.
2. If you're right that there are some individuals who believe they have everything worked out, they very likely suffer from a serious lack of self-awareness, itself a very limiting trait.
3. Don't waste your energy on feeling inferior; instead, invest it in being the best version of yourself.
4. Imposter syndrome isn't all bad. It likely brings advantages that help you do well. If it's debilitating, take account of the opinion of senior colleagues you respect and seek the support of a coach.

You've got this.
Love, Mum x

3.2 Making time for reflection –
and do I need a coach or a mentor?

Dear Joseph,

It's been a theme in these letters that when you're facing difficulties at work, I recommend you take the time to pause and reflect. It feels like much of our culture pushes us towards action so that we risk forgetting the benefits of pausing. Robert Poynton, in his book *Do/Pause – You are not a To Do list*, explains that participants in Oxford University's Said Business School Strategic Leadership Programme value the opportunity to pause and think that this break away from the office affords. And often they value this more than the content of the course they've paid to attend.

Donald Schon has described two types of reflection: reflection *in* action and reflection *on* action. (If you're interested in learning more, there are plenty of explainer videos online.)

Reflection in action occurs *in the moment*. You are aware of what's working or not working as events unfold, and based on your experience and intuition, you take immediate action to improve the situation. This quick problem-solving relies on having a high degree of self-awareness, experience and adaptability.

Reflection on action is more common in the earlier stages of your career when you don't always have sufficient experience to deal effectively with new challenges as they arise. Reflection on action involves deliberate, thoughtful reflection *after* the event. It demands a deeper and detailed analysis of what occurred to find patterns and develop strategies to enhance performance. As I mentioned in *Part 2, Sending and receiving emails*, if you're upset about how something worked out, you should first 'sleep on it' because that can help leverage your ability to process information more thoroughly. Then set aside some time and approach the issue with honesty and a willingness to admit your mistakes.

This is easier said than done, though, because even when we carve out the time, we can lack the discipline to stay focused, especially when the reflection makes us uncomfortable. And it's in those times that I've benefitted from the presence of another mind, whether the issue related to changing my working hours or managing my imposter syndrome. Over the years, I've received help from the mentorship of a handful of senior colleagues, and I've also had some impactful coaching. I'll try to explain the difference between the two.

A mentor is usually a more experienced and senior colleague who has built a career beyond your level and who knows you well. They can give advice and information in response to the questions you ask. They draw on their professional background and experience to answer questions such as whether a specific role would play to your strengths, or if a move to a competitor would be advantageous. They can also advise on handling internal politics. A mentor responds to questions *you* pose in a relationship that can last years during meetings that are scheduled at your request. A mentor encourages action on your part and may use their own network to help you. In short, a mentor will likely help you most with navigating issues in response to questions like, 'This is what I want to achieve in my career here. How can I best progress towards that?'

A coach, on the other hand, may be a person from outside the organisation. They will ask thought-provoking questions that help you gain insight on your preferences and priorities that can inform your next steps. They help you to work on improving your skills to overcome challenges that you identify. A coaching relationship is usually for a fixed amount of time, say, three or six months, meetings are scheduled at regular intervals, and you set the agenda with the coach. The coach should remain neutral and not give advice. Instead, a good coach shines a light so you can see yourself better.

Some years ago, a coach helped me see how I was making myself anxious by expecting the impossible of myself. I realised I was approaching any difficult situation with the expectation that, with enough preparation, I could anticipate every possible scenario. When (inevitably) something unexpected happened, I beat myself up for not being prepared enough. With the assistance of my coach, I could see that when anyone or anything else is involved, none of us *ever* has control. While there is a need to prepare for that difficult meeting or an appraisal, I've learnt that once it starts, I must focus on what is happening there and then, not on what I had planned to happen.

If you want help reflecting on your career or how you're handling yourself, a mentor or coach might be very helpful. Just be clear about what support you're looking for.

Finding the right mentor or coach

In my experience, the best mentors are those more experienced colleagues with whom you've worked and whom you respect. If you've been able to develop a good working relationship with someone like this, they may be willing to mentor you. Just be mindful that they will be busy with their own career, so you should use your time with them wisely by preparing properly for any meeting and being clear about the input you're seeking. In my experience, most people are flattered by a mentoring request, so if you believe you've found the right person to mentor you, don't be shy; ask them. But choose wisely; your mentor should be someone with whom you can be open about your goals.

I once witnessed some mentoring where the mentor, a woman of colour with a generous spirit, was offering advice to a younger woman of the same ethnicity. The mentor was encouraging the mentee to apply for a significant promotion. The mentor was concerned that the mentee's reluctance was due to a perceived cultural behaviour of not 'putting oneself forward'. Indeed, with outstanding appraisals compared to her peers, it did seem odd that this mentee was not seeking promotion. The mentor saw so much of herself in the mentee that it did not occur to her that the mentee might have other reasons to defer promotion. But this was indeed the case. The mentee was planning on starting a family imminently and had decided to focus on that to the exclusion of a promotion, at least in the following year or so. The mentee was not comfortable sharing her priorities with the mentor, leaving both of them frustrated.

If you need a coach, then it can be hard (though not impossible) to find a senior colleague who is happy to stay in the coaching role. After all, coaching is a self-directed activity for you, and a supportive colleague may find it hard not to give advice based on what they would do in your shoes. However, they *aren't* in your shoes, and they can't know what would be fulfilling for you. If you need help with those very personal questions, you may be better off seeking coaching support from outside the organisation, or at least from outside your team. If you are lucky enough to have someone who can be both a mentor and a coach, you need to be specific in your request for help: do you want to be coached or mentored?

Remember ... in making time to reflect ...

1. You need to make a conscious effort to reflect on your performance and progress in the light of your values and priorities.

2. If you don't know what you want to achieve, or you have conflicting priorities, you may find it useful to seek support from a coach, from within or external to your organisation, who can help you find the answers for yourself.

3. If you know what you want to achieve but have questions about how to go about it, then you need advice from someone who has relevant experience, i.e., from a mentor. If you've worked with a more experienced colleague whom you respect, ask them if they'd consider mentoring you. Stay mindful of the time you ask them to commit to you.

You've got this.
Love, Mum x

3.3 The importance of curiosity
– why we need feedback

Dear Joseph,

Too often in school, we're taught that there is a 'right answer' and although over time we become more appreciative of nuance, it can be difficult to shake a nagging belief that in any scenario there is a single right or best answer. And sometimes we feel pressure to *be* that person who has that right answer.

But the world and its people are complex, which means the problems we face at work are often complex too. And because we are human, and we've all had different experiences up to this time, we each have a perspective that is informed by those experiences.

In Rumi's poem *Elephant in the Dark*, the different perspectives of the five men who enter a dark room to feel an elephant are described.[27] One man thinks the leg is a column; another believes the ear is a fan. One man imagines the trunk is a water-pipe kind of creature; another thinks the curved back is a leathery throne, while the fifth man thinks the tusk is a rounded porcelain sword. The thrust of the story is that each person touches a part of the elephant in the dark and cannot fathom the others' perspectives, so they take to bickering, each trying to prove that he and he alone is right.

The human brain can process 11 million bits of information every second. But our conscious minds can

---

27   *https://rumidays.blogspot.com/2010/11/elephant-in-dark.html*

handle only 40 to 50 bits of information a second.[28] To reduce the amount available to a manageable amount, we'll delete, distort and generalise what's available to leave ourselves with the information that we believe is relevant. How we do that will depend on our individual personality and our life experiences to date.

Given the personal approach we each take to filtering, it is no surprise that even if we appear to agree with our colleagues initially, if we dig into the detail of any issue, we are likely to find some differences. That's a good thing because together, we're more likely to have a more complete picture of the issue at hand.

Recognising that there may be other perspectives is a strength, not a weakness. But these perspectives can be hard to hear when the subject matter is ourselves, not least because we cannot know how we appear to others.

Seeing ourselves

In *Part 1, How it's easy to be misunderstood*, I talked about how others can perceive our actions differently to how we intended. Those misunderstandings can make a real difference to the relationships we have at work, and usually not in a positive way. But how are we to know how we come across unless we catch someone rolling their eyes when we speak, or overhear someone complain about us?

We all have blind spots because we can't see our faces or hear our tone of voice when we speak. We are also inherently biased about (at least some of) our capabilities. In well-publicised research, a Swedish study found that an astonishing 93% of Americans thought their driving skills put them in

---

28   *https://online.utpb.edu/about-us/articles/psychology/what-is-cognitive-bias-and-how-does-it-affect-our-lives/*

the top half of all drivers.[29] This study was one of several that proved the same thing: people tend to overestimate their own abilities.

We can't see our own faces

Let me give you an example from my career. I'd been working in the same field for about 20 years and was in a client meeting with some of my team. I had had years of experience dealing with difficult clients. This particular client wasn't on top of his role and when things didn't go smoothly, he was keen to blame others. I had planned to listen calmly to the inevitable litany of complaints about our performance and then agree on our fee without engaging in a back-and-forth blame allocation exercise. Ten minutes into the client's rant, the team member sitting next to me scribbled something in my notebook in front of me.

'Can you stop doing that thing with your face?' As far as I was concerned, I wasn't doing anything with my face. I was, I believed, exuding serenity. 'What?' I scribbled back. 'Your face says he's an a**hole.' In truth, that's what I believed, but I had not intended to share that view. Until then, I had been unaware that my face has subtitles.

Research shows that only 7% of our feelings and attitudes are conveyed through the words we use in spoken communications.[30] Our tone of voice accounts for 38%, and the remaining 55% is conveyed through body language. Although we all like to believe that we control our communication through the words we choose, we need other people to tell us the message we are actually conveying.

---

29   https://behavioralscientist.org/how-to-remedy-better-than-average-effects/
30   *https://www.bl.uk/people/albert-mehrabian*

We can't hear our tone of voice

Once, when I was on a call with a very bright capable junior colleague on a complex project, I muted our line and asked her to run some calculations; she immediately burst into tears. And I don't mean her eyes filled up a bit; she was genuinely distressed. I was busy and distracted at the time and couldn't imagine what I had done to provoke this reaction. She later explained that, based on my tone of voice, she thought that I was angry at her for not having prepared the calculations before the call. That had certainly not been the case and of course I apologised.

But it bothered me that my words could have had such an impact, and I realised that I could well have spoken brusquely on other occasions. Shortly afterwards, I read *Thanks for the Feedback* by Douglas Stone and Sheila Heen. They explain that the part of our brain, the superior temporal sulcus, that is dedicated to taking in language and reading tone and meaning, turns off when *we* speak.[31] The incident demonstrated that because we can't hear our own tone of voice (and especially when we're stressed or busy), we need to be careful of our tone, and we need others to tell us if it's not what it should be. To avoid a repeat of that kind of interaction, sometimes I overcommunicate when making a request, explaining that because time is short, my explanation is brief but there will be time for questions if things aren't clear. Being explicit about the fact that we don't intend to be blunt, for example, can help us keep our tone of voice appropriate and avoid misunderstandings.

We can't see our bigger patterns of behaviour

Finally, we can't see ourselves when we're under stress, for example, if we're struggling to complete a piece of work. We

---

31   Schirmer & Kotz: *Beyond the right hemisphere*: *https://psycnet.apa.org/record/2006-01480-006*

don't realise that we look guilty ('aargh! I've been found out! I don't know where to start') or plain terrified. Our mind races, trying to figure everything out, but our facial expression simply says panic.

If we cannot know these things ourselves, we need to find out by soliciting constructive feedback, and not simply settling for praise. But receiving feedback is not the same as properly hearing it. To experience how you hear feedback, I suggest you carry out a little experiment. Go and ask one of your friends for a small piece of constructive feedback, something you do that irritates them. It's better if it's something small so you don't get sidetracked too much, but the feedback must be critical of you. Observe how you feel (perhaps rate how defensive or upset you feel on a scale of 1 to 10). Notice what narrative comes into your head when you hear it. I think virtually everyone finds it hard to hear constructive feedback. But it's important to know how you react so you can prepare yourself before getting feedback at work. When you know your instinctive reactions, you have a better chance of managing them so you can hear the feedback properly.

We all need to learn to receive constructive criticism and not take it personally.

Criticism is a signal that we need to work on an area. It's just another way to learn. (Learning how to receive feedback well is a difficult skill to acquire, so we'll talk more about it later.) If someone with a fixed mindset has tried but not quite succeeded, they'll be defeated by any subsequent criticism and will believe, *I'll never be any good.* A person with a growth mindset will accept feedback that they didn't get it right at that time; they'll know that everyone fails sometimes, and this is a temporary setback. *I'm on a learning curve. I'll assess what went wrong and try again.* (See *Part 1, Having a growth mindset.*)

Remember ... it's important to be curious ...

1. The world is a complex place, and hearing perspectives that are different from your own is a gift to help you understand the world better.
2. It's usually impossible for us to see or hear ourselves, and that makes it difficult for us to know when our actions are negatively impacting others.
3. The only way to learn how we come across is to get feedback from others, and the first step on that journey is to notice how defensive and upset we get, even when the criticism is minor.

You've got this.
Love, Mum x

3.4 Preparing for your appraisal – helping others to give you useful feedback

Dear Joseph,

You've just received an email confirming your appraisal meeting. You know you've worked hard and done your best, so perhaps you're even looking forward to getting some praise. While that is understandable (after all, who doesn't like to hear praise?), there are two things you must remember. Firstly, if you want to improve, you're going to need to find out what you need to change. That means facing up to the fact that, no matter how hard you work, your performance at work isn't perfect.

Secondly, you will have people around you, like your manager, colleagues and mentors, who want to help you advance. But that doesn't mean they are going to do it for you. You must take personal responsibility for actively managing yourself and your career.

To start improving as soon as possible, you need to actively seek out advice on what you can do better. Remember, this is feedback on the work you've done, not the person you are. Any shortcomings in your performance are an opportunity for you to improve and develop your skills. I've mentioned before (*Part 1, Taking instruction and prioritising tasks*) that if there's an opportunity to get feedback on your work in real time, you should grasp it. When you've handed work over, simply asking if there was one thing you could have done better can elicit useful advice. Hopefully, you've had a chance to do this. In any event, I recommend you read this letter and the next one before you have your appraisal meeting.

Helping your manager to give you useful feedback

You might assume that if your work needs improvement, it's the responsibility of your manager to point that out. Perhaps you feel that you shouldn't have to make much of an effort to get that input. But let's put ourselves in her shoes for a moment.

Undoubtedly, her days are busy, and your appraisal is only one of many things to be done. She's worked with you a bit and you seem nice. She also works with a couple of other junior staff members and, when reflecting on what work was done, she can't remember exactly who did what, and she may not have the time to hunt back through emails to check. She does, however, remember a report she had asked you to draft, which wasn't quite what she asked for. She didn't have time to explain what was wrong with it and so she fixed it herself. Your manager recognises that you're inexperienced and she doesn't want to demotivate you. Also, she recalls giving one of your peers an appraisal last week where she pointed out a few areas for improvement and your colleague became tearful. Your manager decides she can't face you getting upset too. It's much easier to make vague but supportive statements and get this appraisal over with as quickly as possible. If your performance isn't great over the next few months, she promises herself she'll find the time to address it then.

Although it's far from the HR ideal, in my experience, this is a far more common approach to feedback than you might imagine. When it happens, it's rarely because the manager can't be bothered. It's just that she has lots going on, and she doesn't have the time to prepare as comprehensively as she and you might like. Therefore, if you are to uncover some nuggets of advice, you're going to have to help your manager identify them and encourage her to share them honestly with you.

Think about the last time you had to give someone a difficult message. It's likely that you felt uncomfortable. Remember that when your manager is giving you constructive feedback, if you're feeling uncomfortable (or even upset) then she is probably feeling a bit awkward too. Prepare to help her by acknowledging this. 'I know this feels a bit awkward, but I really want to know how to improve, so, please, tell me.' In my experience, actively seeking critical feedback somehow makes it easier to hear.

Reflecting on what you've done

I admit that in the years of giving appraisals, there were times I didn't have a detailed grasp of what a team member had done during the review period. This was not because I didn't care. My workload meant I simply didn't have the time to keep a detailed track of everyone in my team: what they did well, what they could have done better. Inevitably, I relied a good deal on my memory and a few quick conversations with other team members. It was far from ideal. It also didn't help that the appraisal for a review period was often scheduled long after that period had ended.

Eventually, I decided to enlist the help of the people I was appraising. I asked each of them to send me a one-page note ahead of their appraisal, setting out what they'd done, what they thought they had done well, and what they thought they could have done better.[32]

---

32 To have evaluations that are equitable between team members, appraisers should ideally gather evidence independently on the individual's performance and start the appraisal there, only considering a self-evaluation later. In those cases, the self-evaluation is an important exercise in reflection for you. But for those managers who are time-poor and, by appraisal time, have not yet gathered all the information, a self-evaluation will at least inform a conversation where you can learn how to improve, which should be your main objective in an appraisal.

Most of them complained at first and claimed they were too busy to write the note. They struggled to see that this exercise would help me to help them. If they were too busy to invest in their own career, why should I invest my time? We are back to the point that if you want to build a career, you must take responsibility for doing it. I persisted and once the appraisals were complete, they felt our discussions had been more useful because of those notes.

On the one hand, preparing a note like this could seem like self-promotion, allowing you to describe all the great work you've done. That's true, and some people will be better at self-promotion than others. But it's also an opportunity to let your appraiser know the challenges you faced. In my team, I would not have known about the 5am calls required to get the input they needed from the Singapore office on a particular project without being told. After all, it's very hard for a manager to appreciate something they don't know about.

You may baulk at the idea of writing down your shortcomings. Why would you make them conspicuous when you'd prefer to try to fix them yourself before anyone notices? Don't kid yourself. Any decent manager will have spotted your shortcomings already and will be impressed by your self-awareness in identifying them. When she sees that you are prepared to acknowledge your imperfections, it will make it easier for her to point out areas for improvement that you can't identify because of your blind spots.

There is also a chance that you are being too hard on yourself. Until I'd read his one-pager, I hadn't realised that one junior team member felt it had been his fault when things hadn't gone smoothly on a project. He listed all the issues that he believed he should have been able to resolve by himself. He left the appraisal much happier when I reassured him that the buck stopped with me, not him. It was admirable that he was able to see where we, as a team, could improve, but self-destructive to believe that that burden lay on his shoulders alone.

By providing your manager with this information sufficiently in advance of your appraisal for her to consider it, you significantly increase the chances of receiving meaningful feedback.

A word of caution here. Ask your manager if a note like this would be helpful given how busy she is. If she declines, that's ok; she's entitled to her preferences. Nonetheless, it would still be a useful reflection exercise for you before your appraisal so you can get your thoughts in order.

In *Part 1, Taking instruction and prioritising tasks*, I recommended that, where possible, when you've finished a task, you should ask your manager if there is one thing you could've done better. Real- time feedback is immensely valuable, and it's good to make your desire to learn explicit. In the same vein, if your manager offers regular one-to-one catch-ups outside of the formal appraisal process, take them. They're in your interest.

Finally, you may have an appraisal with someone you don't like very much. Whoever it is, they will likely be more experienced than you, and that means they will have some information that could be useful for you. Bear this in mind as your appraisal starts; you don't have to like them for them to help you. In one of my earliest appraisals, my manager was someone I didn't like very much. Technically, she was outstanding, and I could see that she could teach me a lot in that arena. But otherwise (and I'm not proud of this), I saw her as a dull person with no life outside of work. So apart from feedback on my technical approach, I pretty much discounted everything she said, including some advice that I was to receive repeatedly as I progressed. It's not enough to answer the question the client has asked, she advised; you should also try to understand the context. Zoom out, she said. Of course, she was right, and once I appreciated it, I often gave the same advice to others. But I could've learnt that lesson earlier if I hadn't let my personal view of her get in the way of hearing her message.

Remember ... when you're preparing for your appraisal ...

1. If you don't know how you could do better, you won't be able to improve.
2. You are only human; you are not going to be perfect, even if you are doing your best and working as hard as you can. There will be some areas where you need things pointed out to you.
3. Your appraiser is busy. Think about having a chat with them before the appraisal where you can offer to prepare a short note setting out the information I've suggested above. Even if they don't want it, do it for yourself. A structured reflection will help you clarify your thoughts and objectives before your appraisal.
4. You must take responsibility for your career and make it easy for others to help you improve.

You've got this.
Love, Mum x

3.5 Hearing hard things
– how to stay focused on getting value from it

Dear Joseph,

So, did you elicit some constructive feedback from your friend? How did you feel when you heard a small criticism? If you're anything like me, there'll be at least one of the following voices in your head. *That's not true. Who are you to be saying this to me? I'm just not that kind of person.* Sound familiar? And it's hard to hear what someone else is saying when you're busy having a conversation inside your head. Knowing we've done our best and unable to see our blind spots, it's not surprising that our first reaction to criticism is defensiveness. But hard though it is, try to remember that the feedback you receive is about what you've done, not the person you are.

Obstacles to hearing the feedback

It's not true

This is often our first thought. We want to believe that the feedback giver has misunderstood what we've done or is deliberately choosing to overlook part of the situation. We hunt for something that's wrong with the feedback. After all, if we can find something that isn't true, we can give ourselves a reason to discount all of it.

And you may have a point. In my experience, there is almost always something wrong, untrue or incomplete about the feedback we get or give. But there is also almost always something right. If we let ourselves off the hook with an excuse, we miss the opportunity to find the useful nugget that would help us to see ourselves differently and improve.

Who are you to be saying this to me?

Whatever the seniority of the person you report to, one thing you can be sure of is that they're not perfect. Because no one is. That's not a reason to discount their feedback on your performance.

You may have been in this position before. Perhaps your flatmate thinks you leave the kitchen in a mess. Hasn't he seen how it looks when he's been cooking? It's so tempting to become self-righteous and turn the feedback back on the giver so we can dismiss it altogether. But even if it's true that he is untidy, he can still be right that *you* are untidy. While it's tempting to dismiss this feedback, again you are taking an escape route that prevents you from improving your behaviour. Remember, your priority is to improve yourself.

Sometimes our internal dictator rejects the criticism on the basis that the feedback giver just doesn't like us, and therefore her motives are suspect. But her intentions are invisible, and you cannot know for sure what they are. You must set aside her motive and trustworthiness and explore what might make sense about the feedback. Don't forget that those people who are least like you and whom you like the least can give you the best feedback. They have a unique perspective that the people who like you do not have. People who like you can't help you with your sharpest edges because they don't see them.

I'm just not that kind of person

This is a tough one. Because we want to be honest team players, we tell ourselves that that is our identity. We reassure ourselves that we always tell the truth, and we never let other people down. But the truth is, we are all more complex than that. None of us can say, 'I always …' or 'I never …' There are occasions when we have other demands on our time, and we leave a bit early without finishing something. Other times, we find ourselves telling a white lie. Those instances are hard to face when someone else points them out, and so we make an excuse as to why the feedback cannot be right. But while we all get tired, cut corners and forgive ourselves a white lie, it doesn't mean we shouldn't try to improve.

We all need to accept that we aren't perfect, and we make mistakes. If we were perfect, we wouldn't be very likeable, and if we believe we are perfect, that makes it much harder for us to learn.

Getting critical feedback from a good friend (where your relationship can withstand it) will help you recognise and then set aside these defensive voices in your head when you're in the appraisal and your appraiser points out an area for improvement.

Getting feedback that is specific

Feedback needs to be specific to be useful. It's reassuring to hear, 'You've done a great job, carry on,' but it doesn't tell you exactly what makes the difference between a great job and one that is just ok. Is the difference because you always come in early? Or is that irrelevant? Did you do a great job because, having reflected on the instructions, you came back for clarification when you needed it so that your final work product was of high quality? What is it *exactly* that you did that you should do more of? Take notes during the discussion, especially quotes, so that you can reflect on them later as you figure out a development plan.

When we hear criticism, it's tempting to accept whatever we hear (or at least appear to accept it) and get out of that room as soon as we can. It's uncomfortable to prolong that conversation. But if you don't understand exactly what you need to change, how can you improve?

About a year before I was promoted to partner, I was on a business trip with a senior colleague. We were on the flight home when he decided to give me some feedback: 'You need to change how you operate. I don't know exactly how, but carrying on as you are will not get you through to partner.' That felt like the most useless feedback ever. Although I didn't like the headline (that I wasn't going to get promoted if I continued behaving as I was), my frustration was mostly because I didn't know what I needed to change. In hindsight, I don't believe my manager was malevolent. He'd just started a conversation without being prepared. For now, contrast that experience with the very specific feedback I received around trying to show how smart I was (see *Part 1, Your first day*), which was uncomfortable but very useful. (You can find out what I did about this non-specific feedback in the next letter: *When you can't make sense of the feedback*.)

Sometimes, we don't like to probe the person giving constructive feedback; we're fearful that we will appear defensive or that we're trying to persuade the appraiser that she's wrong. Make your desire to learn and improve explicit: 'I'm sorry to hear that. That's not how I saw myself. I want to make sure I understand so I can improve. Can you give me some specific examples, please?' To help your understanding, ask your appraiser what they would have liked to see you do differently. This type of discussion can uncover underlying behaviour that needs to be addressed. For example, you might get the feedback that you need to delegate better. Does that mean you need to give more context, take more time to coach your colleague or something else? A conversation around this could uncover that your development area is none of these; instead, the issue is that more junior colleagues are reluctant to work with you because of your readily apparent high stress levels. Your intensity makes them stressed, even before they begin a task. The development area here is stress management, not delegation per se.

Try to stay curious. Remember that you and your manager may see the same facts in different ways. (See *Part 1, How it's easy to be misunderstood*.) It doesn't mean either of you is wrong.

Remember ... when you hear hard things ...

1. The feedback and the feedback giver don't have to be perfect for the feedback to be useful. Try to silence the voice in your head and look for information that will help you improve.
2. If you don't leave the appraisal with some concrete action steps, it's not because you are perfect, I promise. Perhaps time is short or, overall, you really have done a great job. Even so, it's worth asking: 'Can you tell me one specific thing that you see me doing or failing to do that is getting in my own way?' With a sincere request like this, most managers will usually be able to give you something you can work on. After all, that's your goal.

In my next letter, I'll talk about what to do if you really can't understand the feedback. If you want to read ahead before the appraisal, turn the page.

You've got this.
Love, Mum x

3.6 When you can't make sense of feedback – how to take different perspectives

Dear Joseph,

You've had your feedback, and you can't make sense of it. You're disappointed and frustrated, maybe even a bit angry because you've done your best and the criticism seems unfair. I've had feedback that evoked the same reaction in me, and I know how hard it is to hear.

First, these emotions are a normal reaction, and before you can make sense of what you've heard, you need to let those emotions settle. You might want to vent to a friend outside work, put it out of your mind for a few days, sleep on it … or whatever it takes for you to get yourself on a more even keel. Then you might be tempted to try to forget it altogether. While that's understandable, unfortunately it would likely be a mistake.

So often, I've seen colleagues disappointed they didn't achieve a longed-for promotion and their careers weren't moving in the right direction or at the right speed. I think back to the countless promotion discussions I've participated in. Usually, there was a development area that had been discussed with the candidate in successive appraisals, but no improvement was made, and it eventually became a blocker to further progression. We need to pay attention to what comes up in appraisals, especially recurring themes, and work to understand what we've heard.

Remember, it's natural to look for something wrong with feedback so that we can discount the parts of it that make us most uncomfortable. So, when you feel calmer, ask yourself if there is any way this feedback could be true. Whatever the circumstances, if you don't know how to use this feedback to improve, you need to have another conversation. Don't feel bad about this. Useful feedback often takes more than one conversation.

To encourage your appraiser to help, you want to appear keen to learn, not defensive. Perhaps you've had feedback that your fee negotiation skills need to improve, and you must admit that you're struggling to get a fair price for your work. Is negotiation the issue, or do you have a wider issue with your communication style? Ask your appraiser for help in identifying the area for development.

I had the privilege of working with people who were highly skilled at receiving feedback. They worked hard to understand and apply feedback, trying different tactics and checking in with me to see if I had seen an improvement. Their receptive approach motivated me to help them progress.

Let's look at some specific problems you might encounter in trying to make sense of feedback. Reflecting on these can get you into the right frame of mind to ask for help without sounding defensive.

You believe that the appraiser is missing some key information

Part of you wants to go back in and put it right, explaining what happened. But before you do that, think about whether the information would change the feedback. If not, then why have the conversation? If the information might make a difference, it's important that you find a way to share it without appearing defensive. One way to have that conversation is to acknowledge first those parts of the feedback that you *do* recognise as valid.

Let's imagine your manager gives you feedback that you took too long to prepare a report that required input from, say, the team in New York because you didn't have the local knowledge required. She suggests that you need to be more efficient. You feel that's unfair. The New York team let you down, repeatedly promising you a briefing note but failing to send it for days. When they eventually sent something, it wasn't fit for purpose. You stayed late for three nights, trying to fix it.

If that's the case, then in fact you agree (at least in part) with your manager: the report did take too long to write. If she doesn't know what you went through to produce it, then maybe your pre-appraisal note wasn't comprehensive enough. Perhaps you didn't know how to share what had happened without looking like a whiner about the New York team. And you appreciate that blaming others for shortcomings in your performance can look like you're shirking responsibility.

Remember that you want feedback so you can do a better job next time. This is your goal, more than trying to blame anyone else. But if you just work harder, i.e., do more of the same, this won't necessarily help you produce the next report more quickly. That means this feedback isn't useful to you. You need to have another conversation with your manager.

It could go something like this: you ask your manager if you can have 15 minutes of her time. You've been reflecting on the feedback and want to make sure you can take her recommendations. Start by accepting that the report took too long: that's a fact. Accepting that you aren't perfect and that you have work to do will help your appraiser see that you aren't simply rejecting all criticism.

Explain what happened and ask for her advice to help you do better next time. If you can, offer some suggestions as to how you think you could handle it differently. Should you have gone to her and asked for her advice on how to manage the New York team the first time they let you down? Remember, she can't help you fix a problem if she doesn't know about it. Instead of focusing on why the late delivery wasn't your fault, focus on how you can manage a similar situation better next time.

As a general comment, it's not a good look to blame more junior people in your team for shortcomings in the work you've presented. Your manager won't think well of you, and more junior colleagues will soon avoid working for you. When you delegate work (see *Part 2, Delegating*), remember that you retain responsibility for it.

You can't see past how the feedback is delivered.

You can disagree with how the feedback is given but still learn something from it. I once ran a workshop where a team member, Anna, recalled an incident when she received some constructive feedback from a manager. She recollected that it was delivered out of the blue, and she thought it was harsh. Anna could see that there'd been some truth to the feedback, but her reaction to being spoken to so harshly meant she immediately became defensive. Anna couldn't move past the delivery and focused all her energies on making sure she never worked for that manager again. Anna was certain that he 'had it in for her'.

I suggested to Anna and the group that we put ourselves into the 'third position', as though we were watching the meeting as Anna heard her feedback. Why would the manager be so harsh? Did he actively want to upset her? While it's true that there are some nasty people out in the world, my experience has been that most people don't intend to be mean. (And remember that physiologically we're incapable of hearing our own tone of voice – see earlier in this part, *The importance of curiosity*.) Usually, the discomfort felt by the person on the receiving end is unintended. So, what could have been going on? Eventually, the group decided that one reason for the behaviour could simply be that the manager gave feedback how he liked to receive it himself: directly and to the point.

We are wired for empathy but only if we think the other person is behaving fairly. When we feel harshly treated, our natural empathy and curiosity may be turned off. But if you focus on how the feedback was delivered and use it as an excuse to let yourself off the hook, you have achieved nothing. Pouring energy into your career and improving yourself should take priority over complaining about the person giving feedback. Even if you're right and they intended to upset you, you still win if you can improve your performance using the information they gave you. This can be another occasion when it can be useful to get a third party's opinion afterwards; if possible, seek advice from someone who understands the personalities involved but can still be objective in their advice to you.

No one else thinks I need to change that way

When we are on the receiving end of feedback we don't like, it can be positively enjoyable to have a rant about the unfairness of it all with our friends and have them agree with us. It's even better when other senior colleagues don't give us the same feedback, because then we take comfort that no one else has that view; the appraiser must be wrong.

But it's your responsibility to fix anything about your behaviour that seems to be getting in your way at work. If you can see how you're responsible, that gives you the power to change it. That's far preferable to whining that someone is mean to you.

That's not who I am

In the last letter, you heard about some non-specific feedback I had received: I wasn't going to get promoted carrying on as I was. At that time, I led a small team of eight people that was part of a larger team of eighty. When my initial upset after that conversation had subsided, I went back to my manager and asked him if he could be more specific. After some reflection, he said that he thought I was divisive in the larger team. That was hard to hear. I have (and had) always thought of myself as a team player. He explained that my small team, the people I worked with closely every day, had a strong esprit de corps that helped us work together well. The issue was that I had engendered such a strong identity for that smaller group, it felt exclusive to those who weren't in it. Inadvertently, I had created a clique. Initially, I railed against this feedback. If others felt left out, that was their insecurity, not my actions. Others were envious of our small team's esprit de corps. But a few critical friends were brave enough to tell me they could see the truth in what my manager had said. I didn't need to change what I was doing; I just needed to do more of it with other people. I accepted that I had to work harder at group social events and other gatherings to include colleagues who weren't in my small team.

It may be that you've understood that your feedback requires you to change your persona, e.g., 'be more bullish'. As a naturally quiet person, you feel that you are being told to pretend to be someone else. In such circumstances, ask questions to understand the real issue at hand. Perhaps there is a view that you seem unsure of yourself, or you allow others to speak over you when you're presenting your analysis, and this erodes others' confidence in you. You may need to manage yourself differently, but it doesn't mean you have to handle interruptions by shouting (your experience of bullish behaviour). Instead, you might address the issue by working with a coach or mentor to improve your gravitas in meetings.

You're demotivated; you're never going to be any good at this

When we hear a difficult message, sometimes nuance goes out the window and absolutes reign supreme. 'This always happens to me' … 'I'm just no good at this' … 'I'm never going to get promoted.' Don't allow yourself to stay in this mindset. Instead, if you find yourself 'catastrophising' about the feedback like this, try to right-size it. We are far more complex than 'never' or 'always' anything.

Ask yourself, *What is this feedback about? What is it not about?* Try to stop exaggerating. If you feel like the appraisal was 100% negative, force yourself to recall everything that was said and sort out the comments between appreciative/positive and those that suggest an improvement. You'll reach a more balanced view. In my experience, high performers strive not just for excellence but for (impossible) perfection. In doing this, they tend to skip over and discount positive feedback to focus on areas where they fell short of perfection. If you see this in yourself, it's even more reason to make notes, including verbatim quotes, during your appraisal.

Be specific. Being lousy at one thing doesn't make you lousy at unrelated things. And being poor at something now doesn't mean you'll always struggle with it. Believing that you can't improve can be a self-fulfilling prophecy. Henry Ford said something along the lines of, 'Whether you believe you can or you think you can't, you're right.' It's useful to keep this in mind.

Finally, we can torture ourselves by imagining that everyone spends a great deal of time thinking badly of us. But people spend far less time thinking about us than we fear. After all, everyone has their own concerns to preoccupy them.

Talking it through with a critical friend can help

So many of us listen to opinions that make us feel good instead of ideas that challenge us. And when we're reeling from criticism, we tend to withdraw from everyone except those who will give us comfort. Two biases keep us stuck in existing behaviours. We look for information that supports our previously held beliefs (confirmation bias), and we see what we want to see (desirability bias). One way of helping yourself understand difficult feedback is to ask the opinion of a critical friend, someone who cares about you and who is brave enough to give you their honest unbiased opinion, especially if they know it will be hard for you to hear. Be clear that you want their honest opinion rather than for them to give you comfort. Use the notes you made during the feedback session so that you can provide an accurate picture of what was said.

Remember ... when you can't make sense of feedback ...

1. 'Sleep on it' is good advice.
2. Your goal is to identify areas where you can improve.
3. Although it is cathartic to complain about the person who gave you a tough message, it doesn't help you improve. Instead, seek input from a critical friend.
4. Accept that you can't control how others see you. You can only control how you react – and if you can find a nugget of advice that will help you improve, you will win. And remember that others spend far less time thinking about us than we fear.

You've got this.
Love, Mum x

3.7 Making changes following feedback – what steps to take and getting support from others

Dear Joseph,

Hopefully, at the end of your feedback conversations (the best feedback often takes at least two conversations), you will have discussed with your manager how your progress will be measured and when. A good manager can help you develop by designing objectives that are both stretching and achievable. After all, she will likely have had similar development needs herself or have seen others tackle them.

Setting objectives after your feedback session

Do not underestimate the value of setting targets and timelines for review. Without them, the general busyness of life can get in the way and before you know it, weeks (or months) have passed, and you will have taken no concrete steps to action the feedback. If that happens, there's a risk that, with hindsight, both parties will believe the feedback conversations were a waste of time; you'll still have the same development needs, and now your manager will be less likely to invest in helping you improve.

I mentioned this in the last letter. (*When you can't make sense of the feedback.*) I've seen this happen countless times over the years. An individual would receive the same feedback, year in, year out, but they took no concrete steps towards addressing it. They'd usually give the excuse that they hadn't had enough time to address it since the last appraisal. It was dispiriting for the person giving feedback. Why go to the effort of having these discussions if the person ignores it? Inevitably, it was only when a longed-for promotion appeared out of reach that the individual would take serious steps to address the development issue. But by that stage the habit or behaviour was so ingrained, it took even more effort to address.

Accept that if you have a development area, it isn't going to fix itself. If you don't think you have time to address it, then discuss *that* time management issue with your manager. Ask for her help in prioritising so that you have time to work on it.

Sometimes, the feedback highlights differences that aren't going to go away. For example, compared to your team colleagues who like to get things done ahead of time, you are motivated by an imminent deadline and can only really get cracking under that pressure. In that case, your character is what it is. What you need are strategies to cope with the different approaches within your team, and to develop those, you will need to work with your colleagues to come up with a plan.

Changing is hard work

We often don't realise that because changing our behaviour is hard, it's natural to have a dip in overall performance at first. Developing the new skill may require a lot of effort, leaving less time for your other responsibilities so you don't fulfil those to the same high standards as before. And this dip happens at a time when you haven't yet mastered the new skill. Instead of our overall performance improving, it actually falls off. The risk is that we take stock at this (early) stage and conclude that we should just go back to what we did before, and the development area remains unaddressed.

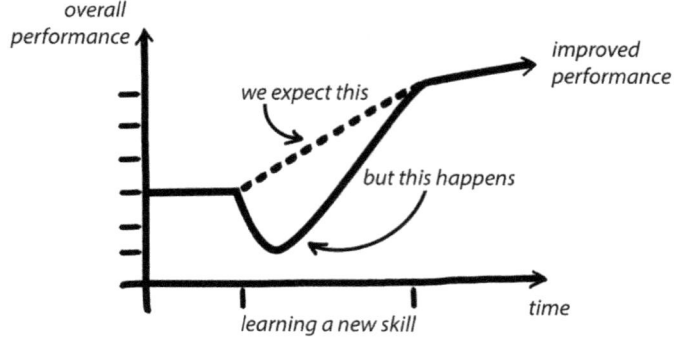

To avoid this, it's a good idea to commit to a plan of action for a fixed period of, say, three months or whatever period is appropriate considering the behaviour you're trying to change. Open communication is vital here. Discuss any workload issues with your manager. It may be that until you've mastered this new skill, you can't continue with the same level of existing responsibilities. Something might have to give, and it's better to plan for that upfront with your manager than try to do everything with less than stellar results. Make your best effort to develop the new skill, but try not to judge your progress until the end of the review period. You might be surprised by how much better you feel then than if you'd judged yourself earlier.

Getting help to change

Sometimes, because of our blind spots, we aren't able to make the change we need by ourselves. I have had this problem. At one stage in my career, when I'd been in my role for quite a long time, I had a very junior team working with me. I wanted their input, but they were very quiet, and I was too impatient to take my own advice of letting a silence be silent. I'd ask a question and if no one answered within five or six seconds, I'd move on, presenting my ideas. Given the team was so junior, it should have been no surprise that they didn't challenge me or present their ideas.

There were a few things I had to deal with. The first was that a junior team member will need to be brave to float a new idea in front of ten colleagues. Secondly, while I like to think out loud (that is, I'm happy to contribute without my idea being fully baked), others prefer to mull something over and only speak once they have worked through the details.

I realised I had to shut up, and for more than five or six seconds. My challenge was to do it. In the moment, I often didn't even realise that I wasn't giving the others enough time to contribute. I asked one of the more senior members of the team to point out when I was 'hogging the ball' of conversation. Admittedly, I had to work hard to persuade them that I was serious about changing and wanted their help to do this. But with their assistance, I improved, albeit slowly.

I also had to make it clear that it would be ok for someone to come back later with an idea they'd been mulling over. If you prefer not to do your thinking out loud, and instead mull things over, I recommend you explain that to your team. There's a risk with silence that they might think you aren't engaging in the discussion, or you're not interested in the outcome.

The point of this story is that if you struggle to identify in the moment when you're exhibiting behaviours you'd like to change, you can ask someone to help you and point them out in real time. Ideally, what you'd have here is a critical friend, a colleague (who could be your manager, a peer or someone more junior) who has your best interests at heart and from whom you are going to be able to take the feedback. Tell others about the changes you're trying to make. Ask them to point out if you're slipping. Be explicit about your request for feedback in real time, so they know they have permission to volunteer it. (See also the letter, *Making time for reflection* earlier in *Part 3*.)

Remember ... when you are making changes following feedback ...

1. Although you should seek support and guidance, *you* are responsible for your career. Work with your manager to come up with specific actions you can take to address your development areas and keep communicating.
2. Changing is hard work so ask for help with time management if you need to, and don't expect a smooth linear improvement in performance. Set a realistic timeframe for assessing your progress with your manager.
3. Don't be shy about asking for help, not just at the start but also ongoing. Show you're listening and trying to improve.

You've got this.
Love, Mum x

3.8 Being yourself – deciding the type of colleague/boss you want to be

Dear Joseph,

By this stage, you've been in the workplace for long enough to figure out which colleagues are good to work with and for. It might be that it takes less effort to please some managers, but you may feel better about the work you do for those people with more exacting standards. You also notice that some people are easier to be with, while you're not sure what to make of those colleagues who seem to play office politics. Taking a bit of time to reflect on how *you* want to behave is worth the investment. Let's start with your core values.

Your core values

Brené Brown, a research professor at the University of Houston, has published excellent work in this area. One of her recommended exercises is to choose two core values from a list of 100.[33] We all want to be honest, competent, confident, look after our family, etc., but limiting the choice to two values forces us to think about what matters most to us. Career progression may be one of your two core values now, but of necessity these may change as your life circumstances change. So, the outcome of this exercise will also likely change over time.

---

33   https://brenebrown.com/resources/dare-to-lead-list-of-values/

In choosing your core values, remember that these should reflect the personal beliefs that guide you when making decisions, building relationships and solving problems both inside and outside work. They are touchstones that can help you decide your priorities at different times.

When I was working in the City and after I had you and your sister, I did this exercise myself. I decided that my two core values were family and integrity. Having family as a core value didn't mean I gave up work or sat at home at weekends waiting for the two of you to need me. But it was a lens that I applied to significant decisions, like whether a new role at work would conflict with my values. By the end of my time in the City, I could honestly say that I had made considered decisions, and although I hadn't been with you and your sister all the time, I had been there for the times that I thought mattered most. On integrity, it meant not taking credit for someone else's work even when the appraisal system would have allowed it. It meant encouraging others on their career path even when their promotion would mean I'd lose a valued member of the team.

In doing this exercise, it's difficult to set aside a value like honesty, but remember this exercise is asking for your two *core* values; it doesn't mean the others aren't important. It's just that they won't be the first touchstone you reach for when you need to make a difficult decision.

Authenticity

Authenticity has been shown to help your chances of making a good first impression.[34] You already know that you tend to trust someone more when it feels like you are interacting with the

---

34   https://hbr.org/2020/02/research-it-pays-to-be-yourself

'real' person.[35] What they say lines up with what they do, and their reasoning is consistent so you can anticipate what factors will influence their decision-making process. In other words, you can see their values in action because their behaviours are congruent with what they say. (See more about congruence in *Part 5, Is this the right job for me?*) In contrast, there are other people whose views change depending on whose company they're in, whose principles appear to be held 'from the teeth out'. In my experience, these people tend to be 'takers', at least in the corporate world. (See section below on 'playing the game'.)

Over the years, so-called personality tests have become ubiquitous. There are several models, such as the enneagram model and Myers-Briggs Type Indicator, which identify personality types or preferences. These models can be a useful framework for discussing work habits and behaviours with your colleagues, especially if everyone in the team participates. But I would counsel you against following it too slavishly. In my first experience with one of those models, I was identified as an extrovert, someone who is energised by being with others. As I usually feel ill at ease in large parties, this extrovert label made me feel there was something wrong with me that I needed to fix. Years later, I benefitted from a more in-depth version of the same analysis (carried out by a more experienced coach), and this time, the analysis pointed to a mildly introverted preference. Immediately, I felt better about owning up to disliking big social events.

Learning from others – the patchwork quilt approach

Once you've figured out your values, you can then reflect on *how* you behave. I found it useful to reflect on what made other colleagues successful, fulfilling to work for and easy to

---

35   The other components required for people to trust you are faith in your judgement and competence (logic), and when the other person feels that you care about them (empathy). *https://hbr.org/2020/05/begin-with-trust*

work with. From this, I decided which behaviours I wanted to exhibit myself.

While it's not a good idea to try to *be* someone else by slavishly copying them, you can still learn from them. For example, I remember admiring the way one of my managers delegated work to me and then let me get on with it. He didn't micro-manage me, but he also didn't mind when I checked in to make sure I was moving in the right direction. He always had time to give me the context for the work he had asked me to do and explain the timeline we needed to meet. I wanted to emulate these qualities but not some of his other qualities, like his reliably poor timekeeping. If you aren't working for or with anyone who has at least some skills you'd like to emulate, do what you can to find a way to work with someone who does. That may mean moving inside your organisation or finding a role elsewhere. (See *Part 5, Is it time to move on?*)

Another of my bosses had superb client-handling skills. I marvelled at how he seemed to be comfortable with saying that he didn't know when someone asked a difficult question. He didn't bluff or answer a different question. He would pause to reflect and then admit that he would need to think about it some more. I was lucky to work with someone else who didn't mind me disagreeing with him; he positively welcomed it and enjoyed the debate. No matter how heated the discussion became, he never took our disagreement personally and our relationship didn't suffer. These were all behaviours I wanted to exhibit with my teams and in each case, it was useful to have a role model. I could ask myself, *What would they do?* if I found a situation particularly challenging.

One word of caution here. Do not take this patchwork quilt approach to your professional role too far. If you build a composite 'perfect colleague' in your head and compare yourself to them, you create unnecessary stress; this version of perfection doesn't exist. For years, I compared myself technically to one colleague whose key strength was his technical skills, to another with excellent client relationship-building skills, to another who never seemed to get stressed, and to another who was incredibly perceptive when dealing with colleagues. It was exhausting because I was always falling short in one area or another. It was more reasonable to have a role model to give me direction rather than expect myself to reach their standards in every case.

Are you a leader?

In my experience, being 'successful' in an organisation often demands the leadership of others, whether formally or informally. Not everyone is cut out or wants to be a leader, so ask yourself, *Can I be a good leader?*

While one can learn how to be a *better* leader, I believe there are two prerequisites for a good leader. The first is that you should have an interest in people. This is not to say you must like everyone; you're only human after all. Second, you should get a kick out of seeing others succeed. If you have those qualities, I firmly believe you can be a good leader, even if you have room for improvement.

When I was working in a large firm and we were discussing key promotions, we asked these questions about each candidate: who is here because of them, and who is succeeding because of them? If there was no evidence for a positive answer in either case, that candidate was probably not a leader. These are questions you can ask yourself if, after a few years into your career, you're working with more junior colleagues. Set modesty aside and be honest. Are you investing in anyone else's career except your own? If not, why not? And how does that answer sit with where you might want to be in a few years?

'Playing the game'

While turning these letters into a book for a wider audience, several people asked if I was going to write about 'playing the game' at work. I understood this to be the practice of networking with senior people who had influence with the sole aim of furthering one's career.

How you behave is a very personal choice and I can only share my approach, which was this. I never 'sucked up', and by that, I mean I didn't build relationships with (or flatter) senior colleagues because of what I thought they might be able to do for my career. I couldn't pretend to like someone just because they might be useful to me. (We've already established in this *Part 3, The importance of curiosity*, that my face has subtitles.) But when I worked for someone I admired, I did my best to learn from them. Sometimes, I got lucky and had a great boss. But not all the time. And on those occasions when I had a boss I didn't respect, I focused on doing the best job I could and otherwise staying out of their way as much as possible until I or they moved on.

And in relation to my peers and more junior colleagues, if anyone asked for help and I was able to give it, then I did. This meant that after a few years, I had a network of 'work friends' with whom I could celebrate any success and who were supportive when I needed help. Throughout my career, I tried to stay true to my core values so that, even when there were bumps in the professional road and I didn't achieve what I wanted to achieve, at least I'd been true to myself.

Adam Grant, in his book *Give and Take*, describes three types of colleague: the givers who help with no strings attached, the takers who help only when it benefits them, and matchers who trade favours in a barter system. He describes a subset of givers who help others in small impactful ways but who set boundaries so they don't get burnt out themselves. These givers don't engage in tactics but stay 'real', building powerful networks where others want to support them. Givers like this, who are selective in who they help so they don't waste time on lazy, entitled or manipulative colleagues, can make great strides in their career. If you're concerned about politics at work, I recommend you read this book.

Remember ... when you're being yourself ...

1. Reflect on your core values and hold those in mind when you're making important decisions and deciding how you want to behave at work, including in relation to office politics.
2. Being yourself doesn't mean you can't learn from others. You can take inspiration from them, but don't blindly copy someone else.
3. Identifying the behaviours in others which make them fulfilling to work with can help you figure out how you'd like to behave.
4. To know yourself better, reflect on whether you have the qualities to be a good leader.

You've got this.
Love, Mum x

PART 4
Having Difficult Conversations

4.1 Preparing to have a difficult conversation – what have you brought to the situation and what is your goal?

Dear Joseph,

Today, you're thinking about having a difficult conversation. It might be that you have someone reporting to you and you need to give them feedback that they are not going to like. You might have to resolve an issue with a colleague who has let you down once too often. Or it could be that the way your co-worker treats you makes it difficult for you to do your best work.

A difficult conversation may be required in any situation where the needs or opinions of two or more people are different and for at least one of them, feelings and emotions run strong. Often, the reason why we feel strongly is that we have a lot at stake, so we dread the consequences of having the conversation. These conversations can be even more difficult if there is a power/ hierarchy differential between the two people.

Learning how to have difficult conversations well means you can prevent tense situations from getting worse. Your conversations can be more productive and improve your relationships in the workplace. And when you're able to hear different perspectives, you have a better chance of coming up with creative solutions together to organisational challenges. (See also *Part 3, The importance of curiosity.*)

Usually, difficult conversations are best handled one on one and in person. This is the case even if, say, there are a number of people who have the same concerns about someone's behaviour. A group deputation feels more like an ambush than a conversation. Although doing it by yourself can be nerve-racking, preparation can help a great deal.

If you want to read more in this area, I recommend *Difficult Conversations: How to Discuss What Matters Most*, by Stone, Patton and Heen (two of whom co-wrote *Thanks for the Feedback*).

Maybe I shouldn't have this conversation at all

It can be tempting to jump to the conclusion that having the conversation is hopeless: the other person is never going to change and you just have to learn to accept it. That may be true, in which case your issue has become one of acceptance, not how to have a difficult conversation. (If the culture of the team is one where open discussion is stifled, it may not be the right culture for you – see *Part 5, Is this the right job for you?*)

Before you decide, consider what will happen if you don't have this conversation. Are you hoping someone else will have it? If you don't have it now, then when? By deciding not to address the issue, be sure that you understand the consequences. Think through the short- and long-term costs and benefits of having the discussion now versus later. Bear in mind that most problems do not resolve themselves, and the situation can get worse the longer you leave it.

What do I want to achieve?

Think about your overall goal. If you want to prevent a bad situation from recurring or to be treated differently in the future, chances are you're going to need to act. While you might see this as simply persuading the other person to change, it might be more helpful to consider how the two of you can alter how you interact *with each other*. You may be able to do that, at least in part, by changing your behaviour. For example, one reason why a colleague never seems to deliver what you want may be because you aren't very clear when you make a request. You may still need to have a conversation with them, but holding the possibility in your mind that you could be part of the problem will influence how you conduct that conversation.

How do I feel about this?

Consider whether the issue has arisen because of what's going on *inside* you rather than what's going on *between* you and the other person. Again, the answer to this may not change your intention to have the conversation, but it may influence *how* you have it.

A few years into my career and recently promoted, I remember my frustration (or was it rage?) when a new team member assigned to help me prioritised a colleague's work over mine. I imagined that the junior had decided that because I was newly promoted, my work could wait. For sure, there was an issue here to be addressed: how should a new team member prioritise their workload? But my reaction to what she had done was at least partly down to my insecurity about how well I was performing in my new role. I was projecting my fears that I wasn't good enough onto her. Taking a few moments to reflect, I realised that, with so little experience of how the team worked, she could not be expected to know how to prioritise her work. I concluded that the difficult conversation I had to have was with my colleague. Between us, we would have to work out a way of helping the new team member prioritise her work. This could still be a difficult conversation, but at least I would be having it with my colleague, who could influence the outcome. And I knew that my sensitivity was at least partly down to my insecurities, something that was not within the control of any colleague.

So, ask yourself, what are you afraid of? What are you trying to control? Perhaps you are trying to get a promotion, so you want everything to run perfectly? But life isn't perfect. Would it be more helpful to seek advice from your manager than to set unreasonable expectations for yourself and your team?

Are you angry about something? Anger can be destructive. It makes us less likely to listen to advice and more likely to behave recklessly and insensitively to our colleagues.

It's so tempting to ignore the emotional side at work but hiding your feelings can increase tension, and then there's a risk you'll explode (or, in my case, cry). And putting off any difficult conversation doesn't help because by the time you finally get round to it, there are then two problems: the substantive issue and the matter of how each person has felt treated up to then.

And don't kid yourself that other people don't have any idea about how you feel. Remember that your tone of voice, your body language and your facial expression convey lots of information. (See *Part 3, The importance of curiosity.*) When a good friend bought me a poster for my office wall which said, 'Did I just roll my eyes out loud?', I was amazed at how many people laughed when they saw it and commented on its appropriateness as a gift for me!

When we face challenges, it is so tempting to wish the circumstances were otherwise, or that someone else would behave in a different way. We complain that no one takes the time to understand us while we are guilty of the same behaviour in return. And the truth is that the only thing we can be certain of changing is ourselves and our reactions to events as they unfold. While that may sound frustrating, it's empowering. By taking the time to reflect on what's important to you, and what issues might be affecting the other person, you can be more deliberate in your actions to improve a difficult situation.

What is the conflict about?

In real life, disputes are rarely about only one thing. Usually, they're fuelled by a mix of tensions. It helps to reflect on what is causing the conflict. Is it a work style, a disagreement over who is in charge or what must be done? Consider when the disagreement started, what you and the other person have said and done, and who else has been involved. Decide what this conversation is going to be about. If there is one main issue, try to focus on that. Throwing in references to other, more minor points can make you look unreasonable, especially if they aren't connected; you'll just look like you're whining.

It's useful to reflect on the stakes for the other person. For example, your colleague could see this project as determining whether he gets promoted, whereas promotion is not on your horizon. In that scenario, the stakes are undoubtedly higher for him. That doesn't mean you shouldn't have the conversation, but bearing it in mind could help you to have a more productive discussion.

When the issue is a difference of opinion on what happened or needs to happen

Surely, you might ask, the facts are the facts? It's just a case of pointing out what the other person has missed and then you can get on with the job, which (let's be honest) is doing things your way.

126

Same facts? Different viewpoint

By changing perspective, it's easy to see something entirely different. It's the same in real life.

Sometimes, it's too easy to assume that you know everything there is to know, and you just need to persuade the other person that you are right. That ignores the reality that the other person may have different information and perspectives that you don't have. Instead of assuming you know everything, you'll do better to hear the other person's perspective and understand why they think as they do. (See also *Part 3, The importance of curiosity*.)

If we are to persuade someone of another viewpoint, we need to understand the other person's view well enough to see how their conclusions make sense. (See also *Part 2, Persuasion*.) Just as our view is informed by how we see the world, what's happened to us in the past, etc., their view is informed by their previous experiences. We need to work on the assumption that there is relevant information that we do not have and make that assumption explicit in our conversation.

Facts, judgements and recollections

Facts are different from judgements. Let's say your colleague arrives at work every morning after 10am. The time at which he arrives is a fact. But if you find your work is delayed because he's not there, you may feel disrespected and might be tempted to raise his lack of commitment to the team. Stop. Your feelings are relevant but they're not an objective fact. We often don't like to admit it, but we *choose* how we react. No one can *make* us feel anything. And your belief that it shows a lack of commitment is a judgement. Instead of confusing feelings and judgements with the facts, it might be more helpful to say something like, 'I like to get in early, but I appreciate that you have a different routine. On this project, I can't get started on my part until you're here, which is usually later than me. Can we talk about this and figure out how we can work better together?' If your colleague agrees to get in earlier but then continues to arrive later, then the issue is reliability and the impact on you. You can reasonably say, 'When we agree on a start time and you don't stick to it, I feel let down and frustrated. Can we talk about this?'

Also, although we like to believe our memory is infallible, studies show that people are not very reliable witnesses even when they are paying attention. Neurological studies show that each time we retell a memory, we rewrite it a little bit as we put it back 'in storage'.[36] If you've been venting to others about this issue, it's highly likely that your memory of the incident in question is not as close to the truth as you might like to think.

There are some things you cannot know

Remember the discussion we had about blind spots? (See *Part 3, The importance of curiosity.*) The fact is you cannot *know* two things: what the other person's intention was or what impact you had on them. (Also see *Part 1, How it's easy to be*

---

36   *https://www.jstor.org/stable/20183151*

misunderstood.) Watch out for when you make assumptions about either of these.

When we're upset, we often infer a malign intention and conclude that it shows poor character on the other's part. Attributions can become self-fulfilling because we behave differently when we think someone has a malign intention towards us. And when we accuse someone of this, they become defensive. When I've taken the time to understand why someone acted as they did, I've found that situations of bad intentions are much rarer than I imagined. Choosing not to take things personally is one of the most impactful habits I have tried to cultivate in the latter half of my career. It has saved me hours of stress and upset.[37]

Add on top that we judge ourselves more charitably than we judge others. In general, we are wrapped up in our concerns, and we are often unaware that we are having a negative impact on others. But we forget that everyone else does the same thing. Remember that you aren't perfect (how dislikeable would you be if you were?), and if you resist acknowledging that you've made a mistake, you will appear insecure.

Don't think that clarifying your good intentions absolves you of your contribution

For years, when I saw that my actions had an unintended impact, I liked to believe that once I clarified my good intentions, the other person would no longer be upset. But I've realised that good intentions don't sanitise bad impact. If it is important that this conversation goes well, prepare to listen to and understand how the other person feels *before* you rush to explain your actions. Explaining your intentions at the start

---

37   More on this and other useful advice in book *The Four Agreements*, by Don Miguel Ruiz.

can make it look like you are more interested in defending yourself than in understanding how the other person feels.

It may be the other person is accusing you of poor behaviour. Unfortunately, the only way past that is through it. You must listen and acknowledge how they feel before you return to what your intentions were. And it may be that, in truth, your intentions were not as wholesome as you might like to think. After all, it is entirely human to act out of self-interest, no matter how objective we believe ourselves to be.

Phew, it is no surprise that conversations can be so tricky.

Remember ... when you're preparing to have a difficult conversation ...

1. Reflect on what your objective is in this conversation, and how you feel about the issues involved. What is the conflict about?
2. If you believe that you know everything you need to know, you aren't ready to have this conversation. Don't confuse feelings and judgements with facts, and don't assume your memory is infallible.
3. There *will* be information you don't have that could change your perspective, such as the other person's intention or your impact on them.
4. Even the best of intentions don't always have the desired impact. Be prepared to hear the other person's perspective before you defend yourself.

You've got this.
Love, Mum x

4.2 Starting a difficult conversation – learning about the other person's perspective and acknowledging your contribution

Dear Joseph,

You've reflected on the work issue at stake, how you feel about it, and what outcome you'd like from the conversation. You're familiar with tendencies that might get in your way of seeing things clearly, like the assumptions you might be tempted to make.

Starting the conversation

Starting can be the hardest part because you'll probably be nervous about how the conversation will go. If it's appropriate, it's not a bad idea to start with something like, 'I'm anxious about bringing this issue up, but I think it's important that we talk about it. We seem to have different views, and I want to understand how we can work better together.' This starts the conversation on an even keel. You need to acknowledge the other person's feelings (and if they are aggressive, remember that their aggression can spring from fear or insecurity). For a productive conversation, each of you needs to feel that the other person has heard what they have to say and is trying to understand.

The third story

In this conversation, remember that you want the two of you to work *together* to resolve whatever the issue is. So, try to describe it in a way that will resonate with both of you; acknowledge that they will have their story, you have yours, and make explicit your desire to understand better. Describe the issue as the difference between your two viewpoints, and invite them, as a colleague, to work on sorting the situation out together. Don't make the other person wrong.

This could be something like, 'David, it seems to me that you and I have different ideas about how to approach this project. I'd like to understand more about how you see it and talk about how I see it.' You aren't giving up your point of view, but you are making clear that you want to understand theirs too. Because you're starting from the perspective of a third party, in Stone, Patton and Heen's book,[38] this is called the third story.

If they've started the conversation (and perhaps they've started it badly with all guns blazing), you need to bring it back to the third story. 'I can see you're upset about that. I have some issues with that too, so it sounds like we have different preferences. It would be good to talk about it and see if we can understand better what's going on.'

And if it's hard to get a word in, try raising your hand a little, as if to wave. That small physical act can be enough to get the other person to pause.

Recognise complexity and nuance

It's easier to see the world as black or white, right or wrong and tempting to see ourselves on the right side. But the world is complex, not black and white. You can feel frustration and appreciation for your co-worker at the same time. Or you may have done something stupid, *and* their actions may have contributed to an outcome neither of you wanted.

---

38   *Difficult Conversations*, by Stone, Patton and Heen

A black and white stance does little other than provoke resistance and defensiveness. So, acknowledging these nuances can only help. I'm embarrassed to share an incident in an early leadership role. Back then, I was adamant that a senior member of the team should turn up to our town hall meetings. I thought his consistent absences showed a lack of commitment and respect to everyone else on the team. In a discussion with him, I paid only lip service to his reasons for not coming and insisted that he should attend. He left the firm within a year. Now it may have been the case that it was the right choice for him to leave, but I'm still ashamed of my dictatorial approach, which I'm sure achieved nothing but resentment.

Look for contribution, not blame

Often, a difficult conversation comes about because things didn't turn out as we'd hoped. As a child of mine, you know that I'm an instinctive blamer.[39] When something goes wrong, I have a regrettable tendency to find something someone did or did not do that fell short of my expectations, which I like to imagine are always reasonable. And, if I'm honest, I focus most on allocating blame to someone else when I'm afraid of being blamed myself. The only thing left after I've made that judgement is to decide what punishment to mete out.

But there are two problems with this approach. First, when I'm trying to avoid taking any blame myself, I'm not focused on understanding what happened or figuring out how to fix it for the future. And when I convince myself that whatever went wrong was entirely someone else's fault, then

---

39   *https://www.youtube.com/watch?v=RZWf2_2L2v8*, an engaging video from Brené Brown on our habit of blaming others.

I have the frustration of accepting that I have no control over what happens next time.

I've learnt the hard way that if I want to avoid a similar situation in the future, I'm better off binning blame and seeking to understand who (including me) and what contributed to what happened. If you can see any streak of a blamer in you, then you too are likely to have a better outcome if you ask, 'Let's think about what happened here. What did each of us do or fail to do that got us into this mess?'

And this is a much easier conversation to have than the blame one. You don't have to have persuaded yourself that you weren't at fault before you start the conversation, and focusing on contribution means you have a better chance of making a positive change. Just because you might have contributed to the outcome doesn't mean that the other person didn't.

Figuring out how you contributed

You can contribute to a problem in more ways than you might want to admit. Maybe you allowed a problem to grow because you didn't address it earlier. Although you complained to another colleague, you couldn't face bringing it up with the relevant person, so they were unaware of it, and you contributed to that. Perhaps you are so busy that you are unapproachable, or you get so stressed that it's difficult for a work colleague to raise an issue with you. Or it might be the case that (like me) your style is very direct, and for someone more reserved, it's difficult for them to raise a problem with you.

On debriefing a role play in business school, I received feedback that I was intimidating to deal with. I was surprised; I like to think of myself more positively as a high-energy person who's interested in other people. But my peers told me that they didn't think I was intimidating because of *what* I said, but because of the intensity with which I communicated. The experience reminded me that I needed to be more mindful of the other person's energy when I was interacting with them. (See *Part 1, Building rapport*, especially the section on matching.)

If you can't figure out how you might have contributed, put yourself in the other person's shoes: how would they say you contributed? Or ask a critical friend (someone who cares about you and you can trust to be honest with you). Be clear that you are looking for constructive input, not comforting noises that it's all someone else's fault.

When I was working in Southeast Asia, we would have several meetings a day, bookended by working breakfasts and client dinners. One trip involved meeting a number of new prospective clients, and the team prepared some briefing notes for me. I asked my assistant to put these with the other information I'd need such as meeting schedules, addresses, etc. When I got to Hong Kong, I pulled out the document wallet she had prepared to read the briefing note in the cab to the first meeting. But there were no briefing notes in the wallet. Instead of printing them, my assistant had attached them to an email. I was frustrated. I couldn't read the attachment properly on my phone and felt unprepared when I met new people on that first day of my trip. My initial instinct was to blame her, but of course, I had contributed to the situation. I had not mentioned that I intended to read the notes in the back of a cab between meetings. Because I was meeting a lot of people, the briefing notes were long, and she had assumed (reasonably) it would be more convenient to have them in email format.

Acknowledge your contribution first

If you can accept that you contributed to the situation, you need to decide when to acknowledge it. If you hold back, the other person can point it out and use it as a shield against their actions. I have found it's better to acknowledge my contribution upfront and then ask how the other person views their contribution. It can be harder for the other person to ignore what they did (or failed to do) when you have been so upfront. If they're still loath to acknowledge their contribution, they likely would have tried to blame it all on you anyway. So, you lose nothing by identifying your contribution upfront.

Don't be afraid to repeat that you want to work *together* to get a better result. Be prepared to say what you would like them to do differently next time. Be explicit and specific.

Remember ... when you're starting a difficult conversation ...

1. Start the conversation from a neutral (or third-story) perspective, and explicitly acknowledge that the other person could reasonably hold different views.
2. Try to resist the temptation to blame someone else for what went wrong. Instead, acknowledge the nuance involved and figure out how you each have contributed to the situation.
3. Acknowledge your contribution and try to understand how the other person feels.
4. Be prepared to say what you would like them – and you – to do differently next time.

You've got this.
Love, Mum x

4.3 During a difficult conversation – mutual caretaking, why breaking it gently might not be a good idea, what to do when the other person reacts badly, and why it is sometimes right to give in

Dear Joseph,

You know that in this difficult conversation, you're going to need to stay curious. 'What information does the other person have that I don't?'

Listen to understand and remember that you can't know some things

I've talked about making explicit your desire to understand better. If you want a different outcome, you won't be able to do that without understanding the situation better and figuring out a way forward *together*. It goes without saying that you need to make an effort to listen properly. Ask questions to understand (without badgering), acknowledge their frustration or upset and, as you move through the conversation, paraphrase to check you've understood properly what they've said. This can be stressful, so remember to breathe! And allow some silence so that your colleague has an opportunity to reflect and say what's on their mind. (If you haven't read it recently, have another look at *Part 1, Listening*.)

Share your story

To facilitate the conversation, it's better if you don't criticise (e.g., 'You take too long to respond to emails'). But it is ok to share why you take the approach you do. Perhaps you're stressed because your colleague operates on a 'just in time' basis. But previously you've worked with someone who was always late, and you ended up having to work through the night; since then, you've always built a buffer into deadlines because you're afraid the real deadline won't be met.

Be clear about how the situation has impacted you, but hold any related assumption as a hypothesis only. Ask the other person to help you understand what is going on. For a colleague who, say, repeatedly misses deadlines, you may feel that that they are giving you the message that they don't want to work with you. So you can say, 'When you often prioritise other work over what I ask you to do, I feel that you don't want to work with me. Is that right?' Be clear about what you are *not* trying to say, e.g., 'It's not that *I* don't want to work with *you*. But I would like us to figure out how to work together better.' If you use the format, 'When you [do that], I feel [like this]', it's less adversarial than a suggestion that someone else *made* you feel a particular way.[40]

Notice more

You should prepare for the conversation and have a plan for how you're going to set out your story. But don't be a slave to your preparations. It's very unlikely that you will be able to predict exactly how the conversation will go, so remember that conversations are a form of improvisation. In Robert Poynton's book *Do/Improvise*, he advises that if we are to improvise

---

40   More on this in *People Skills* by Robert Bolton, now sadly out of print but available from good secondhand booksellers.

well, we need to do three things: let go (of trying to control the discussion), notice more, and use everything. Say you notice that your colleague is nodding their head when you're describing your perspective. You would do well to use this and perhaps stop to check in with them; is this how they feel too?

Mutual caretaking

Remember that relationships that only go one way rarely last, so it's in your interests to ensure that the other person's needs are also met, a behaviour known as mutual caretaking. And remember to talk about how the two of you will keep the lines of communication open in the future so that together you can ensure any plan continues to work for both parties.

When it's hard to listen

In tricky situations, it's common to conclude that the other person is refusing to listen. You end up repeating what you've said, trying to find new ways to say the same thing. (See also *Part 2, Persuasion*.) But, usually, the reason the other person isn't listening to you is that they don't think *you* are listening to them.

And it's true. Sometimes, you aren't listening to them. The voice in your head is commenting on the other person's view, offering rebuttals or highlighting another issue over which you disagree. If you're listening to that internal voice, you can't be listening to the other person. You might try to ignore it, but that internal voice just gets louder. Sometimes, the only way to deal with this is to pause and put down a marker. 'You've just said something about costs. I know we're not discussing costs right now, but I do want to come back to that because we need to talk about it too.'

Or it may be that you simply can't listen or understand because you feel so defensive, it's overwhelming. (See also *Part*

3, Hearing hard things.) The best thing to do then is admit it. 'While I want to understand better what's going on here, I can't help feeling defensive, and I know that that is not going to help us figure it out. Can we pause this conversation and start again after lunch?' Although this might feel like a painful prolonging of a difficult conversation, try to remember that your goal is to reach an understanding you can both live with. Getting to a bad answer quickly is not a good outcome.

You can't control their reaction

Don't assume that the other person likes to receive information the same way that you do. I like messages upfront and crystal clear; don't pussyfoot around me, because I become frustrated and distrustful. Instead, tell me the big picture message so I know the context immediately. However, I've learnt that other people prefer working through the details before getting to the main message. For this reason, it can be helpful to reflect on how the other person likes to communicate before you broach a tricky subject.

However you do it, you have to accept that you won't be able to control their reaction. They have a right to their emotions and for them, being upset might be a reasonable response. So, don't consider your conversation a success simply because the other person seems relaxed or a failure because they got upset. But do show that you care about how they feel and watch out for behaviours from them that won't help in the long term. Unhelpful behaviours include the other person taking a disproportionate share of responsibility for what went wrong, seeing the issue as a complete disaster and taking an 'always' or 'never' approach. Although it might be easier in the moment to accept that route, remember that relationships that only go one way rarely last.

Thinking of breaking it gently?

Be careful when you are communicating an unwelcome decision that has already been made. This is a difficult conversation for different reasons. There is no negotiation here, and no trying to figure it out together. There's a tough message and your job is to deliver it. Breaking things gently can give the other person false hope that a decision has not been made and the outcome can still be influenced. Allowing someone to believe that when it's not true is cruel. You might feel more comfortable, but don't kid yourself that you've helped. You may well have delivered a mixed message. When I've been on the receiving end of this approach, I've left feeling confused and uncertain. So when I have to give a hard message, I believe I have a responsibility to be clear; although it may not feel like it, clarity is kinder in the long run.

You may remember the argument your dad and I had after he had agreed to give notice to one of our childminders.[41] You've certainly heard me remind him of it. (I have a good memory for my grievances!) Giving her notice was time-critical as I had already hired her replacement. Deciding that he would break it gently, your dad lost control of the conversation and because he didn't want to upset her, he ended up offering to 'pick it up again tomorrow'. I was furious. He had achieved nothing. Thereafter, if we ran into insurmountable difficulties with a childminder, I took charge of the communications and would start the conversation with something like, 'Please sit down, Isabel. We're about to have a difficult conversation.' Starting like that meant the childminder and I both knew this was going to be a consequential conversation, and no matter how uncomfortable I became, I couldn't back out of delivering the message.

---

41 Throughout my career, one of the most stressful issues was childcare. The care of you and your sister was a top priority for us and we felt strongly about it. We spent as much as we could afford on it, but occasionally we ended up with less than ideal childcare and we had to start all over again.

What if the other person doesn't want to have this conversation?

The only way to make progress is to schedule time in their diary. For a difficult conversation, you need their undivided attention and a defined amount of time. It will be better if you can do it in person too. Do you remember how much information we impart through behavioural cues? (See *Part 3, The importance of curiosity.*)

You need to be able to show that you've done everything you can by yourself to address the issue at hand. You are coming to the other person because they are the right person to help.

Let's say you've got that meeting, but the other person is stonewalling you. You can ask open-ended questions like, 'What do you think about this?' or 'How do you think we should proceed?' or 'What would you do in my shoes?'

And while we often think that silence is people simply not speaking, we need to remember that silence can be powerful. It allows for reflection. Waiting for two or three seconds can often prompt the other person to contribute to the conversation. Try it at home or with your friends. Ask what they got up to that day and see how a judicious use of silence can sometimes draw someone out more than asking them more questions. Learning this was a revelation for me; I had previously regarded silence as a bowl I had to fill.

When you feel the conversation is just too hard, remember that most difficult conversations are not one but a series of conversations, so it's important to keep communication lines open. Agree when you'll next discuss this issue. Gaining a reputation for not being a pushover generally garners you more respect than giving in, provided you stay open-minded and prepared to acknowledge your contribution.

But sometimes it is right to just give in

Difficult conversations can go round in circles, and the only way out may be to give in. And that's ok when you are persuaded the other person is right, or they care about something a lot and you don't care very much. Perhaps you need an answer at once and, occasionally, any solution is better than no solution. That said, be careful about rewarding bad behaviour, because bad behaviour rewarded gets repeated.

At the end of the day …

Who has time for all of this? Surely, the answer is no one. Everyone has got a 'real job' to do, and these conversations are emotionally exhausting, with no guarantee of a good outcome. It's tempting to focus on less disagreeable tasks, ignore the issue and avoid difficult conversations. But that's a false choice, because the problem won't disappear.

To help you make a more realistic assessment of the choice between having this conversation or ignoring it, admit that you are already spending time and energy worrying about it or talking (venting?) to friends or colleagues. This makes it worse, not better, as our friends are supportive and are likely fuelling our righteous indignation. We might as well use that energy to resolve the issue, and the sooner we deal with it, the more time we are likely to save in the long run. So, prepare yourself, breathe, and start that conversation.

Moving on after a difficult conversation

When faced with addressing a tricky issue with a colleague, we would all like to have one short conversation where difficulties melt away and a way forward is agreed that makes everyone happy. Instantly. But in real life, it can take some time for emotions to settle and a new way of working to emerge. The key to having difficult conversations that are constructive is to keep talking. In the days following a difficult conversation with a colleague, don't shy away from chatting with them about other things. Show that your relationship is more than just this single issue you both find difficult. Not every conversation has to be heavy just because the two of you need to sort something out. Start a conversation as you would with other colleagues; about holidays, films you've seen or even the weather. Just try to ensure that the two of you are communicating as colleagues usually would. It will make it easier when you need to circle back on the difficult issue at stake.

Remember ... during a difficult conversation ...

1. Be clear about how the situation has impacted you without being adversarial, and allow the other person time to air their views. Silence can be a gift.
2. Relationships that go only one way don't last, so take the time to understand what the other person needs and make sure those needs are met.
3. If emotions run high, you might ultimately get to a better outcome if you take a break and restart the conversation later.
4. Often, a difficult conversation ends up being more than one conversation. Although these conversations take time, remember that the issue at hand is already taking up space in your head and time in your discussions with others.

You've got this.
Love, Mum x

PART 5
Where to Next?

5.1 Is this the right job for you?

Dear Joseph,

You've been in this role for quite a while. You really enjoy some of it, but parts of the job are tedious, and at times you feel out of your depth. You're working long hours too and when, consequently, you miss another night out with your pals, you might ask yourself if this is the right job for you.

I thought if I did something I enjoyed, I'd never have to work a day in my life

I stand by my advice that you should build a career around something you enjoy, whether that's rising to an intellectual challenge or helping others, because when you enjoy something you're more likely to excel at it. It was the same when choosing subjects at school. Meg Jay's book *The Defining Decade* has good advice on how you should approach choosing a career. Which line of work you choose is an intensely personal decision, and only you can know what interests you. These letters are not about those fundamental choices.

But what if you've chosen to build a career in an area that genuinely interests you, but it feels so *hard*? Despite its frequent repetition, I don't believe the aphorism that pursuing a career in something that interests you means that you'll never feel like you're working. Keep in mind that *doing anything worthwhile takes effort*, and every job has parts that are less enjoyable or even downright tedious. This may sound unfeeling, but if you're looking for a job that doesn't challenge you and is always fun, you're sure to be disappointed.

I'm working so hard and I'm still out of my depth

Feeling challenged or out of your depth at work doesn't mean you're in the wrong job. It means that what you want to achieve is going to take effort, perhaps more than you imagined.

Think about your goals in your personal life. If you want to eat healthily, you're going to need to make the effort to plan meals, shop for the ingredients and then make the time to cook. When you were learning to play the clarinet, it was fun to play with others in the jazz band, but new pieces were challenging and required slow (boring) practice to get them right. If you want to run a marathon, you won't be able to prepare in a week.

Similarly, getting a dream job in a political consulting firm because you're interested in politics doesn't mean that you're always going to enjoy the long hours in the office or the discomfort of seeing your painstaking analysis demolished by more experienced colleagues. So, feeling challenged doesn't mean you're in the wrong place. *Never* feeling challenged on the other hand would, I believe, mean you've made a poor career decision. Remember that if you're not challenged, you're not learning and you're not developing.

Don't forget that to live a fulfilled professional life, you need to feel that you've achieved something, and that you're improving yourself. That can only happen if you've made an effort over a prolonged period.

I'm working hard but I'm not developing the skills I need

Sometimes, we have found the right career and we like the organisation, but opportunities to develop are limited. Perhaps the organisation's strategy means you don't have the opportunity to work with people who could teach you different skills. In circumstances such as these, where you're clear about the skills you want to build and there are no suitable opportunities on offer where you are, then quitting can be the right answer. Some of us loathe the connotations of 'quitting', and we feel even worse if, to achieve our goals, we must take a pay cut in the short term. In those circumstances, think of your move as a choice and an investment, a positive step you're taking for your future.

There are parts of this job that I hate

Talking to friends and acquaintances from all walks of life has taught me this: every job has parts that aren't fun or interesting. No exceptions. Ever.

I enjoyed each professional role I had, *but not all the time*. I loved working in a team, and I got a kick out of achieving collective success. But there were parts I hated. For example, in leadership roles, I had to attend financial results meetings regularly, which I loathed. The advisory business is all about charging clients for advice, usually by the hour. One particularly dull exercise involved comparing the team's productivity from one month to the next. As we charged by the hour, it mattered if there had been, say, two bank holidays in the review month. To compare like with like, we needed to look at 'days adjusted revenue'. I would have preferred to stick needles in my eyes. But the bonuses and promotion prospects for our team depended on us running a profitable business, so managing and communicating our financial results were necessary evils.

And while I loved helping clients, I hated billing them. Billing required an analysis of the time we had spent advising them, and if the billing period covered a few months, it could be challenging to remember why one issue had taken longer to resolve than another. Colleagues advised me to see billings as a way of me getting paid personally. After all, without charging our clients and collecting the money, the firm wouldn't have the money to pay me. But I didn't find that motivating. But I did find that by billing monthly, it was easier to remember the detail of the work we'd done, and so I could issue our bills with less head-scratching. I still didn't enjoy it, but I made the billing process easier by doing it more often.

Necessary evils are just that: a means to an end. If we can't bring ourselves to enjoy all parts of the job, we can at least consider whether we can take steps to make those tedious parts a bit easier to get through.

Motivation and your habits

When you're embarking on a new project, it can be easy to be excited. You're learning something new and working in a team you love. You're motivated and keen to get started. Six months later, you can't believe how long the project has dragged on. As it winds up, there are only dull jobs to be done. It's February, you're broke after overspending at Christmas, and you're tired of the grey skies and the rain. Whatever you're feeling, it's not motivation.

And the thing is, it's unreasonable to expect yourself to be motivated all the time. Motivation is like the weather, varying from one day to the next. What matters in your professional life, as in your personal life, are your habits. What you do every day matters more than what you do once in a while. Habits such as getting into work on time, listening well and putting in the effort are what will build a strong foundation. Of course, your best on one day (when you're well rested and in good form) may be different to your best on another day (when you're tired and your broken plumbing means you had to have a cold shower). It's the same for all of us. But showing up and making an effort, day in, day out, is what counts.

I can see with hindsight that some of the toughest times I've had equipped me with skills I later found useful. When I first moved to London, I was very lonely for several months until I made good friends. But learning to enjoy my own company during those first few months stood me in good stead when, later in my career, I had to travel frequently for work.

The culture in your organisation

In *Part 3, Being yourself,* I talked about how we trust people whose behaviour is congruent with what they say. We know what their values are and how they're likely to behave in different circumstances. But sometimes we find ourselves working in a culture that is less transparent, where people don't mean what they say, and employees are punished for making mistakes rather than supported to learn so that they don't make the same mistake twice. If you've found that culture in your team, investigate other roles either elsewhere inside the organisation or in a different one. (See also *Part 1, Earning trust* and *Part 5, Is this the right job for me?* and *Taking care of yourself is primarily your job.*)

Remember ... if you're wondering if this is the right job for you, don't forget that ...

1. Anything worthwhile is going to take effort. Being challenged and learning means you're developing yourself, and you're on the way to achievement and fulfilment.
2. If you can't see how you can develop your skills further in this organisation, get clear about what skills and experience you want and find a new role. If a good move career-wise comes with a pay cut in the short term, see it as an investment in your future.

3. All jobs, no exceptions, are going to have parts you don't enjoy. You may never learn to enjoy those parts, and sometimes the best you can do is find a way to make them less painful for you.
4. What you do every day matters more than what you do once in a while.

You've got this.
Love, Mum x

5.2 Taking care of yourself is primarily your job

Dear Joseph,

No one is perfect, and a manager is no exception to the rule. While instances of malevolence are rarer than we think, there are managers and organisational cultures that are toxic. These are people and cultures that place unreasonable demands on their employees time and again. The managers may delight in belittling others, setting one team member against another while rewarding favourites and sycophants. And some managers are unwilling to listen to any conflicting views from their team members, preferring that everyone simply agrees with everything they say. In my experience, such managers are primarily interested in their own advancement regardless of the impact on others' professional development or well-being.

If you find yourself in such a toxic situation, I don't advocate 'If you can't beat them, join them'. Acting in line with your values and your own priorities is key to your self-respect. I have had some objectionable bosses for whom I had no respect, but I did behave so that at least I had respect for myself.

I once worked for someone who gave little direction when he delegated work to me and offered no support when I asked for guidance. He would cast a cursory look over the advice I'd drafted and tell me to send it to the client. I did my best, but I was inexperienced, and effort wasn't enough. More than once, in a meeting where the client complained about the advice, this manager responded by agreeing that I had done a poor job. It was more than stressful; it was distressing.

Eventually, I told him that I thought I needed more training before working with his clients, and then I made sure never to work with him again. I was able to explain to a few of the other managers what was happening and, luckily, they offered me plenty of other opportunities. I appreciate though that, unfortunately, not all roles have that flexibility.

But when any attempt to discuss an unreasonable workload or inequity within the team seems futile, what do you do? If you have tried to have a conversation with such a manager and have concluded it's not possible to improve your situation in the organisation, then you have only two tasks.

The first is to take care of your health, both physical and mental. In my early thirties, I had such an unhealthy approach to work that I believed that if I was at all physically capable of working longer, then I wouldn't be giving my best unless I did. Doing my best meant doing my most. But while there were no prizes for working myself to the bone, there were other consequences. Being so absorbed in work with no real rest meant my judgement was impaired. Small issues loomed large, while I missed the more important ones. Recognising that the quality of my work was falling, I berated myself endlessly. Wherever I went, the voice in my head told me I needed to work longer and harder. I once worked so hard I made myself sick and ended up in hospital. No job is worth that.

An unreasonable manager is unlikely to acknowledge that you're working too hard and insist that you do less. Anyway, you're an adult, and taking care of yourself is *your* job. That means deciding how much work you can do and within what period and then stopping. Setting appropriate boundaries and respecting them is part of the repertoire of a healthy adult. In a situation where you are allocated an unreasonable workload or facing ridiculous deadlines, simply state that you need help to prioritise your to-do list, because you are not going to be able to do it all. Do not apologise for not being able to do more. You are only human, and not a slave. You can remain respectful and polite while saying no to any unreasonable request. It might help to practise this conversation with a supportive friend beforehand, and it's even better if they know what your manager is like. If the workload continues as before, or if more generally the culture is toxic (and there is no way to avoid it by moving internally), you must address your second task: finding another job.

Don't race to take the first position you see; instead, reflect on what you want from your next role, not simply what you don't want.

Once you start to apply for other jobs, you may be concerned that your current manager holds most of the power because they will likely be asked for a reference by prospective employers. And you may also be worried that if you leave after only a short period of time in this current job, your CV will look odd.

In relation to references, there are a few things to bear in mind. In general, prospective employers will not seek a reference unless and until they've decided to hire you. And by that stage, you will have been interviewed and had a chance to explain why you want to move.

So, decide how you want to describe your desire to move to a prospective employer. Honesty is the best option but tempered with restraint. Disparaging your current employer won't come across well, but you can say things like, 'My current job turned out to be very different from how I expected from the interviews,' or 'The team there is very understaffed and there are no plans to address that. Meanwhile, my time is spread so thin that I really am not able to deliver as well as I would like.' Avoid criticising individuals, and describe any difficulties more passively, such as, 'The deadlines are set too tight to allow us to do the best job.' Bring the conversation around to the positive reasons why you want the position you've applied for. In your final interview, if it feels right, you can suggest that if the prospective employer is getting references, you're very happy for them to seek references from your previous employers. Prospective employers will likely be able to read between the lines, and you'll have prepared them for the possibility of a less than glowing reference from your current organisation.

When a prospective employer seeks a reference, unfortunately, there is nothing you can do to guarantee that your referee will behave honestly. But bear in mind that employers are wary of provoking legal action and often limit their written references to the facts, e.g., simply stating the time during which the individual was employed.[42] I can't guarantee you'll get a fair reference though. I've made a few terrible hires in my time, and not one of their referees gave me any cause for concern.

But let's assume the worst-case scenario. The prospective employer wants to hire you but is concerned by what your current employer has said about you. At the end of the day, employers seek strong talent. If an offer doesn't come for this job, you must apply for other positions.

Remember ... taking care of yourself is primarily your job ...

1. If your job is taking a toll on your physical and mental health, remember that these are non-negotiable priorities and you must take responsibility for addressing them.
2. If you can't address the issues inside your current organisation, your next task is to figure out what your next role should look like and apply for suitable jobs.

---

42 Your grandfather once received a character reference for a prospective employee that stated only, 'I have known [John Doe] for ten years. He does not smoke.' No job offer was made. Nevertheless poor references are very rare in my experience.

3. Think about how you are going to explain your desire to leave your current job. Focus on the reasons why you're attracted to the new role and describe any difficulties in your current role passively. Avoid any personal attacks on your current employer/manager.

4. In my experience, poor references are very rare. But if you are concerned about this, find a way to encourage your prospective employer to seek other references in addition to that from your current employer.

You've got this.
Love, Mum x

5.3 Is promotion in this organisation right for you – and are you right or ready for it?

Dear Joseph,

At some point, you'll reach a fork in the road at work and wonder if you should work towards a promotion.

There are broadly two kinds of promotions. The first are those that bring a modest pay rise, but the new role is mostly more of the same kind of thing you've been doing up until that point. This is the kind of promotion where doing your current job well is enough to get promoted. It's easy to go with the flow on this. Your peers are being promoted, and you feel it would be odd if you weren't promoted alongside them.

With the second kind of promotion, the bar is higher because the new role has significantly more responsibility and the day-to-day job is quite different. It takes more effort to achieve this kind of promotion, and you may have to show evidence of different skills before you get promoted. This promotion may also be more political internally (e.g., it might be important to have more senior people backing you for this promotion). It may also be more sought-after, so competition is tough. The rest of this letter deals with this kind of promotion.

Given the extra effort needed, you should invest a bit of time to figure out if you really want it. I must admit that when I decided to try for equity partnership (the biggest promotion of my career at that time), it was far from a considered decision. Some of my peers were clearly on equity partner track, and I thought, *Well, I must be in with a shot if they are.*

I thought leaving without trying to 'make it' would mean I was a quitter. Another reason was that the pay hike would be considerable, and I could easily think of fun ways to spend the extra cash. Finally, I was so busy doing the day job that I didn't think about whether there was another role that might suit me better. As you know, I succeeded, and while I had many good times over the next 20 years or so, there were costs associated with the partnership in terms of the demands on my time and the levels of stress I assumed (and probably shared at home!). I'm not saying I made a mistake. But I do sometimes wonder if a period of reflection, alone or with a coach, might have led me down a different route that might have suited me better. I have no regrets, though, because I spent the greater part of my career working with smart, interesting people who were fun to be with. Not everyone gets to have that.

Success can mean different things to different people. I remember having a discussion with a senior employee who was doing a very good job advising her clients and looking after her team. After some years in this role, she felt compelled to try for partnership, the next promotion. A key difference between the two roles was the business development requirement for partners, i.e., to sell work to prospects, converting them to paying clients. And this colleague hated doing business development. Working in a hierarchical environment, she assumed she had to get promoted or she'd be failing. And, of course, the increase in pay would be welcome too.

However, when we talked about what the promotion would entail, she realised that she didn't want, wouldn't enjoy and was uncertain she would be able to do the business development part of the partner role. In fact, she was pretty sure she'd be miserable doing it. She realised that she loved her existing role and decided against trying for promotion. Had she not taken the time to reflect, she may have invested great effort earning promotion to a job she did not want to do.

You may have some priorities, say, relating to your family circumstances, that mean you need the pay rise that goes with a promotion. Only you can understand the trade-offs you can make. But in reflecting on what the promotion will mean, you can give yourself the gift of having made a considered decision.

The promotion goalposts keep moving

It may be the case that you've been working for this promotion for some time, and it feels like the promotion goalposts keep moving. Perhaps you feel like nothing you do is enough. You've given it your best shot, and you feel like you're ready, but there's always another reason why it's not for you this time. If this is because there are people more experienced 'in the queue' for promotion ahead of you, and you need a fresh challenge to develop, it might be that you need to look at other roles inside or outside your organisation.

Sometimes, the goalposts for promotion shift because of the economic weather or other external factors. Someone higher up imposes a cap on promotions, and your opportunity disappears, hopefully to return next year. But what if next year the result is no different, and perhaps the best you can achieve is a small pay rise but no change in title or role? You ask yourself if you are ever going to get promoted.

As no one is encouraging you to leave the organisation, you're sure you're doing a good job in your current role. But if there appears to be a vacancy for the role you're aiming for, and you're just not getting it, then be honest with yourself. There must be a reason. Have you had repeated themes in your appraisals, encouraging you to work on some development area but you've never had the time to do it? Or is it the case that these skills are outside your comfort zone, and you keep yourself busy, so you have the excuse you're too time-poor to address them? Perhaps your approach in appraisal discussions is to focus on *when* you might get promoted rather than asking the more basic question: does your manager think you will ever make it? If not, why not? Do you make it easy for your appraisers to give you a difficult message? If you are well liked and doing your current role well, it's possible your managers don't want to upset you, so you're going to need to make it easy for them to share their honest views. In this scenario, you might want to ask your manager what they would do in your shoes. Would they continue to try to be promoted or look outside the organisation? You may be surprised at the candour your question evokes.

Remember ... when you're considering a promotion ...

1. Reflect on what the new role will entail day to day so that you can actively decide to pursue the promotion (or not) rather than simply thinking about the money and the title.
2. Figure out if the new role involves activities that you believe you will enjoy. Perhaps those activities will be a stretch for you, but do you believe you can learn to do them?
3. If you don't think you'll enjoy the new role, ask yourself why you're considering it. Perhaps you should be looking for a new role elsewhere, either within this organisation or in another.
4. If you've been trying to get promoted but without success, be honest with yourself about your efforts to address your development areas and how sincere you are in seeking honest feedback, however painful it might be to hear.

You've got this.
Love, Mum x

5.4 Is it time to move on? – think carefully about your motivations, especially if you've been headhunted

Dear Joseph,

Perhaps you are a bit bored with the work you're doing, you don't like your boss, or you feel unappreciated. It might be that others have been promoted and you feel overlooked, or that the promotion goalposts have kept moving. It is inevitable that after a couple of years in one place, you might think about moving on, particularly if you have reached a particular milestone, like reaching a certain level of seniority or earning a professional qualification. Whatever the reason, the novelty of working in your organisation has worn off, and you've been there long enough to have experienced some disappointment.

Often, the impetus to do something about it comes when you hear of a job elsewhere that appeals to you. It might offer more money, the opportunity of some travel or just a fresh start. It's so tempting to rush to move, and it's especially flattering if you've been approached by a recruitment consultant. In that case, remember that it's their job to flatter you and persuade you to move jobs. They only earn a fee when you move, and your personal fulfilment is not their priority. I moved jobs shortly after I'd earned my professional qualifications. I had been frustrated doing some dull work and saw a job in the investment banking sector as more interesting. I didn't realise I was making two decisions: the decision to leave my current job and the decision to accept a specific position in that bank.

What's wrong with your current job?

Some people explain why they left their last job along the lines of, 'I just felt like a change.' I interpret that as either they haven't taken the time to figure out the real reason why they wanted to leave, or they don't want to share that reason with anyone.

To give your career the best chance of success, you need to be honest with yourself. If you want to leave your current job, there is a reason. You need to figure out what that reason is and decide if you can do something to address it in your current organisation.

Often, people move because they believe they deserved, but did not get, a promotion. It's not a bad reason to move, but it isn't always the whole story. The thing is, when you leave, you take you with you. So, if the lack of promotion has its root cause in a development area you haven't addressed, moving job isn't going to cure the cause; the chances are you're going to have a similar experience again. You might manage a pay rise or a more senior title in the short term, but promotion beyond that may be tricky if you don't address that development area.

If you are thinking of resigning because of some aspect of the day-to-day job, say, tension in the team, you may not realise that your dissatisfaction has likely already impaired your performance at work. Compared to how you could perform at your best, you may have made more mistakes, taken longer to complete projects, or your team may have found you more difficult to work with. In turn, these may have affected how your colleagues have behaved towards you in an ongoing reinforcement loop. It's your career and you need to get as objective a view as you can on whatever issues you are facing at work. We've talked before about getting useful feedback in an appraisal. (See *Part 3*.) This might be a time to seek feedback from people whose opinion you respect and who have insight into your performance.

Alternatively, if the problem is your boss or the type of work you're getting, you might be able to solve that problem by moving within your existing organisation. When I left my first job shortly after qualification, I realised within a couple of months that I'd made a mistake. Luckily, my old firm was happy to take me back and agreed to assign me to more interesting projects, a role I could have obtained if I'd asked for it when I was there in the first place.

But the reality is that not every boss you have will be interested in your professional development. I remember a colleague admitting that he didn't like to have anyone on his team who was any better than he was; in fact, he preferred it if they were operating with no more than 80% of his expertise. While this was down to his insecurity, it meant his team members would ultimately have to find opportunities for development elsewhere.

It may be that because of the culture or the lack of opportunity to develop, you can't see yourself in this organisation in, say, five or ten years. In that case, identify the skills you want to develop and the type of environment in which you want to work, and look for another role. Don't hang around hoping against hope that things will magically improve. You owe it to yourself to take responsibility for your career and move to a role that will offer you what you want. This might be something you discuss with a coach or a mentor. (See *Part 3, Making time for reflection*.)

Do you know what your priorities are?

In *Part 3, Making time for reflection*, I encouraged you to make time to reflect on what you want. After all, we can't ask for what we want if we don't know what that is.

I firmly believe that it is very difficult, if not impossible, to have absolutely everything you want at the same time. This means you will have to make trade-offs. (See also *Part 5, Being kind to yourself.*) Some social interests may have to take a back seat in the short to medium term if you want to get a promotion. If you want to work part-time, as I did, promotion at work may not be as quick as it might otherwise have been. You will need to step back occasionally, get clear on your priorities and assess if your choices align with those. It's tempting to pretend that our choices don't have consequences. But it's better to acknowledge those consequences so that, when faced with a choice, you can make an informed decision. (See later, *Part 5, Making difficult decisions.*)

We manage what we measure. If playing football with your old college friends on a Wednesday evening is important to you, keep a note of how often you make it. If your existing show rate is one week in four, perhaps your disappointment is contributing to your overall sense of dissatisfaction at work. Too often, we get sucked into doing the easiest thing in the moment, like staying in the office because everyone else is there. But later we feel disgruntled because we didn't do what we wanted, and the dissatisfaction grows. In this case, addressing with your work colleagues how you could honour your Wednesday evening commitment might reinvigorate you at work.

Leaving can be the right answer

It takes time to integrate into a new organisation, so moving job is not a quick fix to anything. Do not underestimate the effort to build your reputation from scratch, work on new relationships and figure out what is needed to get promoted. You'll already be familiar with your existing organisation, so don't throw away the goodwill, knowledge and experience you've already earned on a whim.

This is not to say that leaving is the wrong answer. A friend of mine had worked hard to correct the initial (less than ideal) reputation she had built. But because more senior people seemed reluctant to acknowledge the changes she had made, promotion seemed unlikely. She moved to a role at the same level in a different organisation. She had concluded (reasonably) that she needed a fresh start. Although moving was a good decision, it wasn't without risk. She would have to invest in new relationships, and there was no guarantee of advancement. But those risks were dwarfed by those associated with staying, where her efforts seemed futile. It was uncomfortable for her to recognise that she had contributed to the dynamic in her first job, but that reflection helped her figure out how she might get off on the right foot in her new role. She was more self-aware, and moving was the right decision.

In another case, a young man I had worked with extensively announced his resignation the day after he had achieved a significant promotion. Naturally, I was disappointed, and for a short time I was also angry. I had invested a lot of time in helping him get the promotion, and I felt he had let me down. But our business was structured in such a way that specialists advised on different areas of the law, a practice he found restrictive and unfulfilling; he wanted to work across a broader area. When I stopped thinking of myself, I realised he had done the right thing for him. In a similar way, if you want an opportunity to take on greater responsibility and, say, lead a team, you may decide to leave if where you are means those opportunities won't be available for some time. (Also see later, *Part 5, Making difficult decisions*.)

How you leave is important too. Aim to be a good leaver. In the future it's likely that you'll interact in some way with your soon-to-be former colleagues, and it doesn't help if you tell everyone what's wrong with the organisation/the team/them on your way out. You can of course be honest in your exit interview, but stay measured and try not to say something in the heat of the moment that you might later regret.

Remember ... if you're thinking of moving on ...

1. Before looking around for new jobs, figure out what isn't working where you are and whether it can be addressed without you having to move to a new organisation.
2. Talk to a colleague you can trust to be honest and discreet. Check your perspective on what's going on. Are you contributing to the dynamic that you find so dissatisfying?
3. Figure out what you want that you aren't getting in your current job. Moving can be the right thing to do, but be as specific as possible before you consider new positions. Will they meet your needs?
4. Moving can be the right answer. In that case, aim to be a good leaver; you never know when you'll come across your former colleagues again.

You've got this.
Love, Mum x

5.5 Being kind to yourself – when there isn't enough time, you might want to practise intentional imperfection

Dear Joseph,

There will be times when you feel stressed and overwhelmed, rushing from one thing to another and making decisions on the hoof. We can be very unkind to ourselves at times like these; we beat ourselves up for not getting through our to-do list a bit quicker. It's tempting to turn to books, podcasts and the like, searching for help increasing our productivity.

Productivity

It's fair to say that most of us could have a few better habits regarding productivity. We'd get more done if we focused on one task at a time rather than keeping one eye on our phone or email. Studies show that switching tasks can reduce productivity by 40%.[43] And the constant flow of information via emails, social media and news alerts means we never seem to have enough uninterrupted time to really think. So, yes, paying attention to how you pay attention is a good idea, and it's possible to get more done when you stay focused.

But that's only going to get you so far. Because, as you build your career, see your friends and family, take care of yourself and keep on top of household admin (laundry doesn't

---

43   https://www.apa.org/topics/research/multitasking

do itself), you're just going to have too much to do to do it all well and in less time. To squeeze more into the day, you might try to cut back on sleep and soon discover that being exhausted doesn't help. You miss the buzz from working out and your skin shows the ready meals you've been 'preparing' in the microwave. And you can hear your short temper in your interactions in the office and at home.[44]

Intentional imperfection

It might be time to embrace the concept of intentional imperfection. Perhaps, if you had the time, you'd like to see your old friends from school at least once a month, cook your meals from scratch, produce excellent work in the office and get to the gym three times a week. But when you've got too much to do, you have to accept that something is going to have to give.

And it's better for you to decide what takes priority rather than responding to the push and pull of those around you; meeting everyone else's needs and few of your own will likely leave you feeling exhausted and out of control. One approach is to view your to-do list through the lens of 'do what *only you* can do'. A good friend of mine who has a very demanding job admitted that he's let himself off the hook in relation to taking his elderly mother grocery shopping. His sibling lives nearby and can easily do it. However, sorting out his mother's pension requires financial acumen, something he can take on but is outside his sibling's skillset. My friend does what only he can do.[45]

Sometimes, other life events mean that our best effort at that time is far from what we are used to achieving. Perhaps

---

44 For more on this, read Oliver Burkeman's book, *Four Thousand Weeks*.
45 See *https://seeyourfolks.com/?ref=parents-are-human.ghost.io* for an app that estimates how many more times you will likely see your parents based on their age and how frequently you see them. I'm not sure it's reliable, but it is thought-provoking.

we have suffered bereavement, there's a serious illness in the family, or we have pressing financial concerns. At these times, we can be kind to ourselves by admitting that it's just not possible for us to do what we usually do. Please share your difficulties with your manager. Perhaps there is nothing they can do to help, but if they know the challenges you're facing outside work, they're better placed to support you and perhaps cut you some slack. There's no gold star for struggling on your own and collapsing from the effort. Keep communicating so that when the situation has been resolved or is otherwise less demanding, you can let your manager know that you're now able to focus on getting your contribution at work back on track.

Trade-offs

If you can afford it, spend a little money to make your life easier. In my first year of working, I preferred to spend to have my shirts ironed (I hated ironing, and my efforts did not look good), which meant I had less money for socialising. I was happy with that trade-off. When I was expecting you (my first baby), another female colleague at work gave me this advice: 'For a working mother, the most stressful thing is childcare, no question. Spend as much as you can afford on it even if you must cut back on other things.' She was right. While holding down a demanding job with long hours, the most stressful part of my life was when the childcare arrangement wasn't working.

Some trade-off decisions may have a short timescale, e.g., I won't have time to go to the gym this week because I have a lot on at work and it's my friend's birthday, or a longer-term effect, like my decision to work part-time when I had school-age children. Having less money was easier for me to accept than the fact that any promotion would come more slowly.

I recommend you talk through more long-term decisions with someone who has your best interests at heart, whether that's a family member, friend, coach or mentor. I think it's impossible to overstate the benefit of having another mind alongside yours to work through the implications.

Communication

When you've made your decision and other people are going to be impacted, you need to let them know sooner rather than later. For some people, you might want to explain your reasoning. For example, if you're rehearsing with your jazz group for a big concert, explain to your manager at work that you can't miss your Tuesday evening band practice. When I asked to work part-time, I explained to my then boss that my life felt like a pressure cooker; I was rushing between home and work, especially as your dad was travelling a lot at that time.

But it's likely that the people to whom you owe an explanation are fewer than you think. If you struggle, as I did, to say no to other people's demands, you might find helpful guidance in *The Courage to Be Disliked* by Fumitake Koga and Ichiro Kishimi. This book relates five conversations between a young man and a philosopher during which we learn that each of us is in control of our life's direction, independent of past burdens and expectations of others. While all relationships require give and take, it is not our job to fulfil everyone else's needs and disregard our own. To right-size others' demands on our time, it can be helpful to discuss competing demands with a neutral third party. Someone once berated me, 'I can't believe you're so selfish that you won't do what I want.' Only later in the retelling of this to someone else did I appreciate the irony.

Being intentional about what takes priority brings two benefits. You're more likely to make progress in your priorities because you aren't spreading yourself so thinly, and you can be kinder to yourself about the lack of progress on those goals that you've decided are lower priority for that period of time.

Remember ... to be kind to yourself ...

1. If you're feeling overwhelmed, you're not alone. Almost everyone feels they have too much to do and too little time. Increasing your productivity will only get you so far.
2. Apply the lens of 'doing what only you can do' and work out if you can afford to spend a little cash to make life easier.
3. Be intentional about your priorities over the short and long term. Deciding that something isn't a priority for now allows you to let yourself off the hook in that area and makes it more likely you'll make more progress on your priorities. Reflect on who needs to know about the decisions you've made.
4. When you're making these decisions, it can be useful to talk to someone who has your best interests at heart.

You've got this.
Love, Mum x

5.6 Asking for what you want –
being imaginative and brave

Dear Joseph,

In my last letter, I talked about taking the time to figure out your priorities. Waiting for someone else to see your problem, diagnose it and suggest an effective remedy is wishful thinking. Only *you* can know what you want. But even if we've decided what we want, often we conclude that the only way to get it is to change jobs. Why is that?

A failure of imagination

Exhausted and stressed, it's easy to admit defeat. 'What's the point in imagining how things could be different here? This is the way things are.'

Time and again, I've watched colleagues decide they want something a bit different and assume they must leave the organisation to get it, even though their current job meets their other needs. 'There's no point in asking,' they say: they believe they have to do their job based on how others have done a similar role. They cannot see a different path, regardless of the not insignificant effort needed to move to and then thrive in a new environment. It feels easier to resign than articulate a different vision to superiors and colleagues.

But I have also seen colleagues who dared to imagine a different way of doing their job and succeeded in being allowed, sometimes actively encouraged, to do it their own way. Take Sarah, who began to hunt for a new job because she no longer wanted to work the long hours that had already taken a toll on her health. She believed that her supervisors would prefer her to leave than to remain in the team with a reduced workload. When she finally told her colleagues of her plans to leave, she was delighted to find that they much preferred her to stay in an altered role with reduced responsibilities than leave the team completely.

A year or so into my first job in London, I decided I had to leave because of the long hours. I said to myself, *Surely, they must see how hard I'm working. If they wanted me to have a future here, they would see the difficulty I'm having.* I had failed to understand that 'they' (my managers) were busy trying to get their own jobs done and simply hadn't noticed how miserable I had become. I did start a resignation conversation only to be offered the chance to join a new project team in the same organisation. I loved it, and although it was hard work, I had more time off. But not everyone is so lucky. They resign and, at best, their employer tries to persuade them to stay by rubbishing their new job rather than discussing how to improve the one they're leaving.

We are afraid to show ourselves – what will others think?

If you want to change your working practices, and you're part of a team, it's likely that any change will affect others. It can feel daunting to open up to colleagues and superiors to articulate what you need to lead a fulfilled life.[46] One can't retract a heartfelt statement if the listener doesn't want to engage in the discussion.

Before you decide against having this conversation, ask yourself if what you want is so unreasonable. Just because no one has done it exactly as you want to do it doesn't mean

---

46   Only you can determine what fulfilment looks like for you. Figuring out your core values, *Part 3, Being yourself* might help.

that your approach isn't possible. How would we ever do anything new if we boxed ourselves in with what has been done before?

Most of us worry about what other people think. When I catch myself in this trap, I remember that when I become immobilised by others' views, I'm allowing their opinion of me to be more important than my own opinion of myself. But a shift in perspective to consider what my life will look like in x years if I keep doing what I am doing right now can give me the confidence to have that conversation.

Brené Brown, a Research Professor at the University of Houston, describes a way to think about this concern for others' opinions in her book *Daring Greatly*. She recommends that each of us decides whose opinions of us matter. Think of it as deciding who sits in the royal circle in the theatre of our life. (In a theatre, the seats in the royal circle have the choicest view of the stage.) Figuring out whose view is important, why their view matters to us and whose views can be discounted takes a bit of effort. On the one hand, there are those from whom permission is necessary, and on the other, there are those colleagues, family and friends whose respect and goodwill you want. When I started doing this exercise, I allowed myself ten seats in my royal circle though that number has become a good deal smaller the older I get. My immediate family took up three (you, your sister and your dad). That left seven for colleagues and friends who had my best interests at heart (rather than, say, the interests of my employer). Your royal circle might be bigger or smaller but don't let it get too big, or it defeats the purpose. It is a relief to concern yourself with what only ten (or fewer) people think.

One weekend, some time ago, I watched your then toddler sister hold a toy phone to her ear as she stood in front of her teddies. She explained to the teddies that they had to be quiet because she was working. Observing that was a wake-up call for me. I realised she was imitating me. Even when I was physically present with her, I was often unavailable because I was checking my email or calling the office. Officially, I was working a four-day week at the time, but I often spent time on Fridays answering emails or joining work calls. Although I loved my job, in the theatre of my life, my children, now as then, sit in the royal circle. I wanted to spend more quality time with you two. In a few short years, she was going to join you at school and then what would I do on Fridays? Work more? Join school coffee mornings? I concluded that I wanted to revert to a five-day week during term time but take unpaid leave during the school holidays, something that no one in my role had ever done. That would give me quality time with the two of you. This working pattern required permission from the firm's leadership, the active co-operation of my team who would have to cover in my absence (although holiday periods are generally quieter, there would still be extra work for them when I was out), and acceptance by my clients of my unavailability at certain times.

I had to decide whose opinion at work was important, either because I needed approval or because I valued their input. Planning these conversations was key. I had to be honest about how I saw the choice: I had to change how I worked or find a job elsewhere. Happily, the colleagues whose opinions were important to me were wholly supportive of the change, believing the team was better off with me in it, even for a shorter time, than out of it completely. Although some colleagues abhorred my unusual working pattern, my career advanced and my periodic absences gave valuable opportunities to more junior members of my team who benefitted from greater client exposure. It also allowed me regular periods of reflection, which helped me think of new ways of doing things at work.

Sometimes, you may find that the person whose permission is needed cannot or will not engage in the issue you are trying to resolve. That may be because their life priorities are very different from yours and they don't understand your position, or they're simply not interested. Whatever the reason, in such circumstances, resignation may be the right answer. That said, in my experience, most employees are surprised by the support they receive, once they've dared to ask for it.

Time spent reflecting on how you can do your job so that you thrive is time well spent. Having a fulfilling job and a balanced life that serves us facilitates valuable relationships at work and at home. Pay your future self the respect of taking the time to figure out what you want and how to get it.

Remember ... you need to ask for what you want ...

1. Just because no one has done your job the way you want to do it doesn't mean you can't do it differently.
2. If you don't ask, you likely won't get what you want.
3. If you've done your best to get what you want where you are (and that means explicitly asking for it) and you've made no progress, the right answer may be to resign.

You've got this.
Love, Mum x

5.7 Making difficult decisions

Dear Joseph,

So, you have a difficult decision to make. Perhaps you are mulling over whether you should accept a job offer, change your specialist area, join a new team or move to a new city. We can't predict or control the future, so an outcome, however desired, can't be guaranteed. We can, though, be thoughtful about how we make decisions to give ourselves the best chance of making good ones.

Making the decision

You've taken the time to reflect on your goals, and you know what your key values are. You've gathered as much information as you can and, where appropriate, you've taken advice from a mentor and thought through the pros and cons of each option. The issues remain complicated and nuanced. It could be that the pros and cons seem to balance each other out, so there's no clear logical 'best' choice. Or maybe the pros of one option materially outweigh the cons, but still you don't *feel* good about choosing that route.

Research shows that intuition is a key tool in decision-making, provided it is used appropriately. The Nobel Prize winner Daniel Kahneman addressed the problem of recruiters relying heavily on intuition when assessing candidates. He recognised that relying solely on a recruiter's initial impression or intuition was a flawed and unreliable approach. He believed that intuition, while seemingly quick and effortless, can be easily influenced by biases and personal experiences, leading to inaccurate judgements. You've probably heard of biases such as confirmation bias (we look for information that confirms our opinion and disregard that which contradicts it), availability bias (we think an event is more likely if we can easily recall something similar) and the affinity bias (we gravitate towards people who we perceive are like us).

To overcome this, Kahneman designed a more structured interview process that involved defining relevant, specific and measurable traits like punctuality, gathering concrete information about those traits and then scoring candidates on each of them. However the recruiters were loath to ignore their gut instinct entirely, and Kahneman found that intuition was indeed useful *provided* the recruiters delayed using it until *after* all objective data were collected. Using this approach, Kahneman significantly improved the predictive accuracy of the recruitment process.[47]

So, in making a big decision, instead of discounting the importance of our emotions, we should actively take them into account, but only *after* we've done the more objective analysis. When I've been in this position, sometimes I've been overwhelmed with contradictory emotions. I only knew what I really felt about a choice when I tried to articulate my feelings, whether that was in writing a journal or in response to a question from an engaged and interested friend. Although I don't recommend choosing between two options by flipping a coin, if you don't know how you feel, flipping a coin and noticing your reaction when it lands might help you find out.

Executing the decision

The outcome of a decision is impacted by the quality of our decision-making, which is why we invest so much energy in

47   https://www.ted.com/podcasts/daniel-kahneman-doesnt-trust-your-intuition-transcript

making our choice. How motivated we feel about that decision will influence how we execute it. Again, our emotions play a key role in our motivation as those emotions inform the story that we tell ourselves (and others) about the decision and the outcome we expect. In other words, if we decide to pursue a specific route but our 'heart isn't in it', when obstacles inevitably arise, we're less likely to work hard to overcome them and more likely to give up. Instead, we tell ourselves that our decision was the wrong one to start with.[48]

Let me give you an example. After a few years working in Dublin, I had a relationship with a colleague. (I know, it wasn't smart, but if you're working long hours, the chances are you're going to meet someone through work.) Anyway, things didn't end well, and I concluded that our small office wasn't big enough for both of us. My decision to leave was easy. The hard part was deciding whether I should work with another firm in Dublin or move to London. I drew up a list of pros and cons. Staying in Dublin was an attractive option; I had already made friends, I knew the city, I had built a specialism in Irish law and, although it was early days, I had a decent reputation. But there were disadvantages to staying in Dublin too; the economy was booming but wages hadn't kept up with inflation. My dream of owning a flat was becoming less achievable. I'd been visiting Dublin since I was a small child, and part of me hankered after new surroundings. London would give me a fresh start, new surroundings and a better salary. But it was a bigger market with more competition, I would miss my friends, and I would have some catching up to do. Irish law was similar to the law in the UK, but not exactly the same. I might feel like I'd taken one step forward and two steps back. For complex and nuanced decisions like this one, a simple list of pros and cons didn't help.

---

48   *https://www.gsb.stanford.edu/insights/more-feeling-keys-making-right-choice*

Ultimately, I *felt* moving to London was the right decision. I didn't expect the move to be problem-free, but I was confident I could overcome whatever challenges arose, and there would be the upside of living in a large and vibrant city. Who knew what opportunities might present themselves? I was very lonely for the first six months, finding it harder to make friends in London than in Dublin. But my limited social life, especially on workday evenings, meant I had time to read up on the technical areas where I lagged my peers. Having uprooted myself with a narrative that ultimately the move would bring me success and happiness, I was determined to stick with it. Moving back to Dublin was not an option I would consider.

And therein lies an important truth. If I hadn't been so deliberate and considered in my decision to move to London, I suspect I would have spent the first few months in London wishing I was back in Dublin, instead of putting my energy into making my move work. Sometimes, we invest so much energy in making what we call the 'right' decision that we forget we're going to need to put in effort to make that decision right. And we're more likely to be motivated to do that when we've gone with a decision that *felt* right.

Baba Shiv, a professor at Stanford Graduate School of Business, explains that once we've set an expectation, we are more likely to find evidence to support it. He tells the story of an experiment with subjects being invited to a wine-tasting.[49] They were told that they were going to try five different wines made from the same grape variety which sold for different prices. The researchers monitored the individuals' brain activity and found these registered more pleasure from wine described as more expensive, even where the wine was *the same* as a cheaper wine that they also sampled. He describes it

---

49   https://www.sciencedaily.com/releases/2008/01/080126101053.htm

as, 'What you expect, you manifest'. In my case, I expected to make a success of my move to London and (eventually) I did.

Nevertheless it's important to take the time to reflect on your progress periodically rather than blindly following a plan and ignoring information that might indicate you should make some changes. But how you make your decision, the story you tell yourself about it and the expectations you set for yourself will all influence the outcome.

And something to bear in mind: research shows that in the long term, the mistakes we regret are not errors of commission (things we do) but errors of omission (things we don't do). If we could start again, most of us would be braver.[50] Ask yourself upfront, *What's the one thing that, when I look back in 12 months' time, I'll regret not doing now*?

Remember ... when you're making a difficult decision ...

1. Check back to your overall goals and values. How does the decision you're facing line up with those?
2. Gather as much information as you can and think through the pros and cons of your options. Once you've done that, take the time to figure out how you *feel* about each option.
3. With the pressure of making a consequential decision, it can be hard to know how we feel. Go for a walk, write it out or talk it through with an engaged and interested party (ideally, one who doesn't have a personal preference for one option).
4. Once you've made the decision you feel is right, focus your energy on making that decision right.

You've got this.
Love, Mum x

---

50   *https://pubmed.ncbi.nlm.nih.gov/7965599/*

And finally …

Dear Joseph,

So, that's it. I've passed on everything I can think of that might be relevant to you as you build your career. Undoubtedly, you will face challenges that I have not imagined. I have no silver bullet.

But I will leave you with this quote from Bertrand Russell. 'In all affairs it's a healthy thing now and then to hang a question mark on the things you have long taken for granted.'

Stay curious, Joseph, about everything. This is especially hard in a polarised world where there's a constant challenge to pick a side. But life is more nuanced than that, and certainty is the enemy of understanding.

You've got this.
Love, Mum x